After
Life

What it's like in Heaven,
Hell, and Purgatory

by
Michael H. Brown

Published by:
Faith Publishing Company
P.O. Box 237
Milford OH 45150-0237
U.S.A.

The publisher acknowledges that since the abolition of certain Canons of the former Canonical Code, publications about new apparitions, prophecies, miracles, etc., are allowed without an express *imprimatur*, providing they contain nothing which contravenes faith or morals. Regardless, the publisher herein wishes to submit to the final judgment of the Holy See of Rome.

The Publisher

Published by: Faith Publishing Company
                          P.O. Box 237
                          Milford, Ohio 45150-0237
                          United States of America

Additional copies of this book may be acquired by contacting:

For book stores: Faith Publishing Company
                          P.O. Box 237
                          Milford, Ohio 45150-0237
                          USA
                          Phone: 1-513-576-6400
                          Fax: 1-513-576-0022

For individuals: The Riehle Foundation
                          P.O. Box 7
                          Milford, Ohio 45150-0007
                          USA
                          Phone: 1-513-576-0032
                          Fax: 1-513-576-0022

Front cover illustration: **Christian Wilhelmy**

To the souls in Heaven and Purgatory, please pray for us all.

Acknowledgments

I'd like to thank all those who shared their experiences with me, as well as those who worked on the manuscript. I thank Mary Ann Reck Liming for her support, and Bonnie Lewis for her most capable editing. I would also like to thank those others who work with such dedication at Faith Publishing and my wife Lisa and her parents for enduring yet another intense project. God's peace now and for eternity!

Chapter 1

It's the greatest of all questions and it's with us every moment of life: What happens when we die? What happens when we leave earth? What is it like in eternity?

No question is more important. No answer has larger consequences. Whether or not we know it, we've been preparing since birth for what comes after life. Our entire existence is but a build-up to death, and everything we have ever done, anyone we have ever known, and anything we have ever seen stand as mere preface.

Earth is but a stage of life and throughout our earthly journey we harbor the often daunting notion that one day we will all succumb to aging, an illness, or accident that will release our souls into a world that is vastly different. One day, at a time we can't foresee, and in a way we're not allowed to know, we all die. We all leave this planet. No human escapes that fate. Some may try. Some may build castles in the sand. Some may accumulate all possible wealth in a way that looks like they've conquered the world (and thus immortality), but in reality every person is equal and every single person will arrive at a point when his or her soul is brought into the eternal.

No matter who you are and no matter where you have been, no matter what you or others think of yourselves—no matter how highly or lowly—one day you'll be a naked soul before God and the way you're judged may surprise you. It may be a shock. But the sure thing is that it will happen. Death will come. So will judgment. The princess with her wardrobe, the glamorous Hollywood actress, the tycoon with his portfolio of stocks and bonds: all die. All meet the same end. At the conclusion of their days, all must face eternity.

No human has avoided it. No amount of money, no amount of political power, no level of "genius" can change the simple fact that while on earth humans are of a physical nature and as such will eventually perish. One day you will be reduced to nothing but spirit. One day you will shed the physical vehicle we call the "body" and move into a spiritual dimension. If you're prepared, it will be a glorious day, a day of indescribable joy, a day of the greatest release and freedom. For upon death we enter a world where there is no longer time and there is no longer death and there is no longer a blindness toward the Lord.

If you're prepared it will be great beyond your wildest imaginings. It'll be better than anything you could wish. No fantasy could contain what God has in store for you. It will make the worst suffering on earth seem like a trifle—the tiny price of admission.

That's if you're prepared.

If you're not prepared, eternity will be another matter. For in addition to Heaven there are also Purgatory and Hell. I know some of you don't want to hear this, and I know it's not often preached, but since infancy we have all been heading on a road that leads to one of those places. We may try to engineer our immortality. We may try to change it. It never works. It never will. Death will always come and we will be sent to one of the three places. *Which* place depends on how we conduct our lives, and it's never too late. No matter how you have sinned you always have hope, right to the last second. Throughout history God has granted many clues as to how to gain the best afterlife. He has shown how to conquer death. He has shown that death loses its sting for those who follow Jesus (*1 Corinthians* 15:55). It should even be *joyous*. It's what Christ called "good news." What a wonderful truth! And what a surprise: Death doesn't have to be the morbid spectacle our society has built it to be, for when we reach a spiritual state, the fear of it, the fear of the "end," turns into anticipation and joy.

Chapter 2

Christ came to remind us that we're spiritual and not physical beings and that our consciousness does not cease upon earthly death.

We do not "blink out."

Our existence does not turn into nothingness, despite what certain philosophers say.

Earth is temporary. It lasts but seven or eight decades. And that's a grain of sand on the beach of eternity. While on earth we're in exile. We're away from home. We're on a mission and we're in a kind of school and we're being tested for something much larger than anything you can see with your eyes or hear with your ears or even imagine. I don't think there could possibly be better news than that: after death there is life. The soul doesn't end with the body. Our bodies are not us. Our *souls* are us. One day we'll look at our earthly bodies as nearly foreign matter when we find our true selves in the spirit world at a time of fantastic wonder.

That's the news of Jesus. After death there's another existence and if we prepare, it's a splendid existence, an incredible existence, an infinite situation that will engage us for all eternity.

Death is a transition. It's a shedding of the physical shell. It's the transcendence of a body which had been used as a sort of instrument in the physical realm. There is nothing to fear if we have Jesus. There is nothing to fear if He awaits us. In fact, when scientists have studied the attitudes of dying patients, they've been amazed at the large number of people who, in the hour of death, are happy and even *elated*. There was evidence, said one study in New York, "that considerable numbers of patients meet death not with fear and despair but rather with elation and exultation."

The fact that death is less intimidating than many think was shown clearly by the way Jesus endured the worst possible death, only to quickly rise above it. If there was one lesson from His Resurrection, it was that the supernatural exists and the spirit moves beyond the body. We also see descriptions from Paul, who in *2 Corinthians* 12:4 said, "I know this man— whether in or outside his body I do not know, God knows— was snatched up to Paradise to hear words, which cannot be uttered, words which no man may speak." Elsewhere in the Bible we're told that "eye has not seen, ear has not heard, nor has it so much as dawned on man what God has prepared for those who love Him" (*1 Corinthians* 2:9).

Since the time of the caveman there has been belief that the human soul is transcendental, and it's a belief that is common to every people and culture, in every age, no matter how modern or primitive. From the beginning of recorded history people have had experiences that indicate the eternal nature of the soul and in our own time, with reports of apparitions and other religious phenomena, we have only seen an affirmation of those ancient beliefs.

The soul lives after death. It cannot be destroyed. It is not made of a physical substance. It exceeds anything physical. In fact, it *controls* the physical. It controls your body. And upon death it moves on to eternity. It heads for its true home. Those who are dying in the grace of God sense this—sense their homecoming—and know they are at the end of a difficult and dangerous journey.

Physical pain and the reliance on money—the bondages of flesh that make life one constant struggle—end with death.

There's no more limitation.

There's no more doubt.

And contrary to the greatest of fears, there is no "nothingness." We do not go blank. Our Blessed Mother reminds us of this at her famous apparition site in Medjugorje. *"You go to Heaven in full conscience, that which you have now,"* she said on July 24, 1982. *"At the moment of death you are conscious of the separation of the body and soul. It is false to teach people that you are reborn many times and that you pass to different bodies. One is born only once. The body, drawn from the earth, decomposes after death. It never comes back to life again. Man receives a transfigured body."*

Such is also borne out by those who claim to have had what they call "near-death" or simply death experiences. From time to time, I'll be using the testimony of certain people who have "died" and come back to tell what it was like. Today we are privy to many such cases because of modern techniques of resuscitation, especially in cardiac arrest, as well as improved rescue services, that allow us to "bring back" those who would otherwise have met their deaths. And in case after case—in thousands of reported instances—those whose hearts and lungs have stopped, whose brain waves stop, who show every sign of departure, describe leaving the earthly body and what they encountered afterward. According to George Gallup, Jr., the famous pollster, a survey in the 1980s showed that as many as eight million Americans had some kind of otherworldly experience during a brush with death.

The most recent survey by the American Sociological Association has indicated that 81 percent of the American public believe in life after death. The polling figure for Catholics is the highest this century and without a doubt some of it comes from the accounts of death.

That's certainly a good fruit, but we have to be very careful and discern such experiences just as we must carefully discern apparitions. Let me stress: We must be cautious. Some of the most prominent cases of after-death encounters have involved New Age or other questionable and even occult lingo. That's the unfortunate interpretation of many non-Christians who have the experience. They don't have the proper context, and in grasping for a way of viewing their incidents, they wander into pop religion. They put their own erroneous spin on it. Some even promote channeling and reincarnation. Just as there are questionable apparitions of angels and Mary, so it is true with death experiences. "These postmortem visions can be looked upon as good, but we can't go beyond that," said Monsignor Corrado Balducci, a theologian who lives in Rome and specializes in demonology and the paranormal. "We might consider them the *grace* of God. But we should not look for them. God wants faith from us."

Death experiences are not the main reason we should believe in life after death.

But many of them ring of authenticity and many of them resonate with goodness. They confirm what was said at Medjugorje: that at the moment of death the soul is removed from the body in full realization of the dying person.

Chapter 3

Consciousness survives. What joy it is to know our God is so good that He has formed us to live forever! No matter how difficult and depressing life may seem, no matter how sad a situation may appear, there is always—literally—a light at the end of the tunnel!

But before we view Heaven we must realize that life is a test, a trial, and a battle. Every minute counts. We're put on this earth to claim Christ's victory. Every minute we're given tests of our love, humility, and trust. Every day we face trials to see if we've gained patience and long-suffering.

Every day we're given opportunities to avoid the traps of Satan and advance toward the virtues of Jesus.

When we think of life as one big test, it becomes all the more meaningful. It makes more sense. It becomes exciting. When we see life as a challenge, those who suffer can comprehend their sufferings and those in pain—any kind of pain—now see it as a mere test that precedes eternity.

The problem in our times is that we try to find a material paradise. That's not in God's plan. There is no earthly utopia. Try as we might, we'll never find perfection in the physical. Such thinking is a deception at a time of great deception, and at a time when mankind is on an incredibly materialistic course.

Life is a test. Everything about us from the moment of conception to our final breath is watched closely by Heaven, and at every juncture there are events that may seem minor or even trivial but can carry tremendous meaning.

The people we meet, the locations in which we live, the work we do, the relatives we have, and the places we go, are all rich in meaning. Every aspect of life counts. God doesn't play with dice. There are no coincidences.

And there is no superiority. Everyone on earth is equal. Everyone is equally loved by God. Everyone is given tests and sufferings (though some sufferings are more visible than others), and everyone has the same chance to use the incredible opportunity of life to gain a splendid *after*life. Every moment is terrifically precious because every single thing we do, think, or say counts with God.

We don't have this opportunity forever. Life goes by in a flash. While it may seem that seven or eight decades are a long time, to God a thousand years are like a single day (*2 Peter* 3:8).

Think about it. An average person lives about 912 months, or in the area of 27,750 days.

Let's break it down further and express it as approximately 665,000 hours or perhaps 40 *million* minutes.

Think of the things you can do in a minute. Think of the number of thoughts you can have or words you can say.

Every tick of the clock counts, and forty million minutes further reduces to 2.4 *billion* seconds.

That sounds awesome, but to God such figures, such numbers, are child's play. To a God Who can keep track of every single living creature on a planet, with nearly six billion people, and trillions of other life forms right to the one-celled amoebas (and Who can also keep track of billions of other stars and planets), keeping track of our lives is certainly no big deal.

And that's what He does: He keeps track of every single thing we ever do or say. He even records our thoughts. He watches everything that passes through our minds and monitors what we hold onto and what we reject.

We'll get to more of this later, but it points out the responsibility we have for the priceless time we're given on earth. Every moment that we live has tremendous potential for good or evil and every moment of life brings us closer to or takes us farther from God.

Every minute counts. We can pray in that moment, we can love in that moment, we can praise God in the tick of a clock, but we can also latch onto a hateful or lustful or otherwise damaging way of thinking and detract from our eventual judgment.

My point is that God wastes nothing and not a single thing we do is meaningless. God isn't a cruel God. While death seems terrifying to us, once we look back from the afterlife we'll see that it's not a bad thing. It's nothing to fear. In fact, as I said, it should be a happy experience. If we're prepared, if we live the rest of our lives as God wants, if we're in tune with the Holy Spirit, it's not only a pleasant experience but an exhilarating one.

From the moment of birth all of us are given countless opportunities to do good and at the end of our lives, in a way we cannot fully perceive, God will instantly analyze how we have handled ourselves each of those 2.4 billion seconds and how much we have purified ourselves, how much we have risen above Original Sin. He will evaluate how much we have helped reclaim what Adam and Eve lost.

Life on earth is transient and passing. To find the best place in the afterlife, let me repeat, we must prepare every waking moment. There is never a second to lose. We need to start right now—this minute. Earth is merely a testing ground. We're not to obsessively hold onto any aspect of personal life any more than we hold onto an old grammar school classroom. Every day, in many ways, we find ourselves tested. We're tested for our faith. We're tested for our humbleness. We're tested for our patience. Most of all we're tested to see how much we love. With each personal trial our spirits grow and we have that much more understanding. With each successful trial we gain brighter heavenly apparel. It awaits those who have fought the good fight and who have loved Jesus.

There is nothing to fear for those who have followed His teachings.

Heaven is an incomparable joy, and most of us will one day reside in it.

As the *Catechism* says, "This mystery of blessed communion with God and all who are in Christ is beyond all understanding and description."

There have been glimpses of Heaven and I think you will find them astonishing.

Chapter 4

But before we consider Heaven, we have to face other realities.

There is Purgatory, where the majority of souls go for purification before entering into God's presence.

It's not a Catholic myth. It's a fact. Everything points to it.

There is also that netherworld—that horrible place—of Hell. It too exists.

And before we view Heaven we must look at those two destinations.

We must also view the process and joy of death itself.

What do they say happens at the moment of death?

The experiences of those who have "died" and come back vary but have much in common. As death approaches, many people have visions or apparitions of departed relatives. Friends they haven't seen for decades are suddenly in their thoughts and dreams. When my grandfather was dying he would peer with wonder into thin air and say, "Look at all the old-timers!" It was as if deceased friends were stopping by.

Is it hallucination and delusion? One classic study tabulated the responses of many physicians and nurses who have observed deathbed patients. In breaking down 884 cases of what seemed to be visions during terminal illness, this study found that 86.7 percent of those experiencing visions or mood elevations were clearly conscious and that most were *not* under sedation or delirious. Patients were described as elated or appearing surprised as death approached, their eyes wide as if staring at something. The visions could last minutes at a time and seemed to have a very calming effect.

Those dying reported apparitions of the Sacred Heart or of "people dressed like they did at Christ's time."

Others saw angels and saints, including the Blessed Mother.

Still others saw Jesus.

Such apparitions join those of deceased relatives who come to help at this critical time.

While anxiety and fear as well as pain may be present in the days leading up to death, such usually disappear one to three hours before departure and are replaced with comfort and peace.

There is no terror for those who reside in Christ.

"Surprisingly enough, *fear is not the dominant emotion in dying patients* according to the opinion of both physicians and nurses in our sample," said the study. "A hospital staff physician commented: 'There is such a resigned, peaceful, almost happy expression which comes over the patient—it is hard to explain but it leaves me with the feeling that I would not be afraid to die.' "

In one sample of 15 whose mood at death was described as "exultation," 13 were found to have religious affiliations and the study noted that "one woman, while kissing her rosary, died radiant."

Now remember: these are scientists talking!

In another case a nurse reported a bright light that appeared for two seconds as a patient died and there was also the case of a nurse who witnessed the same apparition as her dying patient.

Similar things have been recorded elsewhere. Among Protestants is Billy Graham, who said a light illuminated the room as his mother passed away.

Often, there are angels. An oncologist at Yale University reported that a seven-year-old girl who was in the last stages of leukemia sat up just before she died and said, "The angels— they're so beautiful! Mommy, can you see them? Do you hear their singing?"

Many who have themselves crossed the threshold say that at the instant of death their spirits were suddenly removed from their bodies. The next thing they knew, they were "floating" near the ceiling. Often they describe watching from above as the nurses and doctors fervently tried to revive them. Or they watched as relatives mourned their passing. I've even read the account of a doctor who contracted typhoid in 1889 and left his body during a coma, walking around the room trying to get the attention of his wife and sister to assure them he was okay, as they wept inconsolably over his corpse!

He had no recorded pulse for four hours.

"I recollect distinctly how I appeared to myself— something like a jellyfish as regards color and form," this doctor later recalled. "I floated up and down and laterally like a soap bubble attached to the bowl of a pipe until I at last broke from the body . . . I saw a number of persons sitting and standing about the body and particularly noticed two women apparently kneeling by my left side, and I knew they were weeping. I have since learned that they were my wife and my sister . . . I now attempted to gain the attention of the people with the object of comforting them as well as assuring them of their own immortality. I bowed to them playfully and saluted with my right hand. I passed about among them, also, but found they gave me no heed . . . I concluded the matter by saying to myself: 'They see only with the eyes of the body. They cannot see spirits. They are watching what they think is me, but they are mistaken. That is not me. This is me and I am as much alive as ever.' "

Once out of their bodies, the deceased not only maintain consciousness but seem to feel more awake, more conscious, than ever. They describe leaving the physical body as a surprisingly smooth, painless, and easy experience. In some cases they report exiting the body in the instant just *before* a fatal accident. Way back in 1892 a fascinating study of thirty mountain climbers who survived nearly fatal falls found that an astonishing 95 percent of them had felt calm during their experiences. There was no grief or pain or fright.

Instead, there was a supernatural presence.

"The process of dying," said the study's author, a Swiss scientist named Albert Heim, "is far more frightening to onlookers than it is for the dying themselves."

It seems the death experience begins with a sense of well-being and soon culminates into a feeling of ecstatic joy.

The dead are light as air. They are given what Paul described in *1 Corinthians* 15:35-52 as "celestial bodies" and there may be a sound like buzzing, like the wind, or like heavenly music.

Those who die in frightening accidents seem to transcend fear. Upon parting they may see their bodies dying and bleeding, they may see the daunting and graphic circumstances, but there's no horror.

Chapter 5

Whisked outside their physical bodies, the deceased remain in the immediate environment for a short time and see their own bodies from somewhat of a distance. Those whose experiences occur in a hospital describe the things that were said and worn by the nurses, the instruments used by the doctors, and the reaction of relatives in the waiting areas—things they simply could not have known through the use of physical senses, since their eyes were closed and they were unconscious. In some cases they knew what was being said or done in their homes *miles away*.

And no matter how grisly or painful death seems to the onlookers, it is most frequently described as free of pain and in fact a total joy. It's a journey to their real home. It's freedom.

In one case a housewife from Bismarck, North Dakota, went into a coma after gynecological surgery and suddenly found herself watching the nurse from outside her body, like a movie. She later recounted: "I understood that the Christian promise was real. Christ was with me, God was with me, and there was nothing to be afraid of. In fact, were it not for the anxiety of my family [who she could see], I would have felt wonderful, because I felt at peace not only with myself, but with my God."

As surprising as it seems, many describe dying, in the words of one survivor, as "the most wonderful, worry-free experience you can imagine."

Another such person said, "Since this experience I don't fear death. Those feelings vanished. I don't feel bad at funerals anymore."

This is also in agreement with the messages of Medjugorje, where the Blessed Mother has promised that . . . *"if you abandon yourselves to me, you will not even feel the passing from this life to the next life. You will begin to live the life of Heaven from this earth."*

One woman who had visited Medjugorje and was dying of cancer saw an illumination as she neared death. So did her mother, who recounted, "She raised her head and looked at me, her starry eyes full of suffering, then laid her head back on my breast. I felt I was holding a bundle of peace. She seemed to be asleep. Suddenly, a great hush or stillness descended on the room and I felt that time stood still. I could not move. I felt I was frozen in time. Have you ever been in a room by yourself and someone came in and although you did not hear or see them you felt their presence? I felt the presence of royalty and I felt that Jesus, the King of Peace, and Mary, the Queen of Peace, and their attendants had come. I felt a great awe.

"Suddenly I saw a flash of a bluish light and then a clear form came from my daughter's head and went up and disappeared. I saw the movement as it went up. It was surrounded by a golden light with a thousand tiny twinkling lights. I don't know if the lights were around the golden light or on it or in it. It lasted only two or three seconds and then disappeared. I looked down at my daughter and saw that she had died."

Those who experience death describe moving through a vacuum or dark passageway, a tunnel similar to what was once described by seer Vicka Ivankovic of Medjugorje during a journey to Heaven. "It wasn't exactly like a tunnel," she noted, "but a tunnel is the closest comparison." Those who enter it recount a sensation of being whisked at great speed toward the light of eternity. One man described his experience as so powerful "I almost floated in it. It was feeding my consciousness feelings of unconditional love, complete safety, and complete, total perfection."

Recently I met a former police officer and devout Catholic named Paul Limas from Omaha who had a similar account. "Approximately eight years ago, I suffered an attack of Bell's Palsy," he said. "I was treated with steroids. My kidneys stopped functioning and I went into congestive heart failure. My blood pressure was 260/180 when I reported to the emergency room. I was a 48-year-old former professional athlete who had never been sick. On my way to the intensive care unit, I was told that I should be dead from stroke or heart attack.

"I went into surgery immediately. Tubes were placed in my lungs and a tracheotomy was performed. During the testing in the recovery room of the fit of the tracheotomy, the doctor had me cough as hard as I could. When I did, the trach tube tore loose and shot out of my throat. Blood was everywhere and I was choking. I remember being catheterized as I was being wheeled back to surgery.

"The doctor told my wife that I might not survive another shot of anesthesia. The next thing I remember is a sensation of total awareness and a golden light. I was aware that Jesus *was* the Light. The joy and love I felt were indescribable, the feeling of total awareness and freedom of all restraints, like a genie freed from a bottle. There was no tunnel but there was the sensation of very rapid movement toward the light."

Such accounts are not unique to our time. Many after-death accounts were recorded by Pope Gregory the Great in the fourth century. While as I said we must be careful that such experiences are not deceptions (which occur in every kind of mysticism), or simple artifacts of the imagination, the indications from Medjugorje and historical cases of Catholic phenomena point to many of these experiences as valid and the quality of witnesses further bolsters the credibility. As in the case of Paul Limas, once out of the physical body there is often a beautiful and holy light. Many are those like George Ritchie who in describing their experience explicitly state that "the light which entered that room was Christ. I knew because a thought was put deep within me, 'You are in the Presence of the Son of God.' I have called Him 'light,' but I could also have said 'love,' for that room was flooded, pierced, illuminated by the most total compassion I have ever felt."

Chapter 6

Just as in apparitions of the Virgin, who appears in a similar luminosity, the light described at death is far stronger than the sun and yet never hurts the eyes. Instead, it's restful and comforting. In the sixth century St. Salvius, Bishop of Albi, was believed dead of a fever but recovered consciousness and described "being taken by two angels and carried up to the height of Heaven, and it was just as though I had beneath my feet not only the squalid earth, but also the sun and the moon, the clouds and stars. There I was brought through a gate that was brighter than our light, into a dwelling place where the entire floor shone like gold and silver; there was an ineffable light and it was indescribably vast."

As Pope Gregory added, "Anyone who has seen a little of the light of the Creator finds all of creation small, because the innermost hidden place of the mind is opened up by that light, and is so much expanded in God that it stands above the world. In fact, the soul that sees this is even raised above itself. Rapt above itself in the light of God, its inner powers are enlarged. When it looks down from above, it finds that what it formerly could not grasp is now small."

Often angels are also encountered, including Michael, Raphael, and Gabriel.

St. Bede recounted the story of Drythelm, a pious man who died one evening after a severe illness but was revived the next day at dawn. He said when he left his body he was guided by a man "of shining countenance and bright apparel" who escorted him to an enormous valley (which reminds us of *Psalm* 23).

The same happened recently to a lawyer who was in a helicopter that plunged into a river. I know of this case personally. While hovering between life and death he was guided by a being who asked if he wanted to come or return to earth. There were many praying for him. He chose to return.

Others are guided by the Blessed Virgin. Shortly before the death of St. Clare the Blessed Mother visited her with a multitude of virgins in snow-white garments.

The same was true of St. Stanislaus. He saw Mary with a band of angels.

When St. Hyacinth died on August 15, 1257, a holy nun saw him being led to Heaven by the Virgin.

And then there was Padre Pio. His very last words were: "Jesus . . . Mary . . . Jesus . . . Mary," and he died with what the attending doctor said was a look of incredible sweetness.

Chapter 7

While death is usually pleasant, not everything is sheer bliss. There are times when evil spirits come as a final trial. In the writings of Pope Gregory is the account of a soldier named Stephen who upon death crossed a bridge over a gloomy black river with foul-smelling vapor. He had to get by there before reaching the fragrant meadows.

This is why it's important to invoke both Mary and the Archangel Michael. This is why we must have a direct connection to Christ.

While so many recount death as the most pleasant experience of their lives, we must always be on guard against the evil one.

"At that last decisive moment, the devil lets loose all his rage against the one that is dying," said one 19th-century revelation to a nun in France. "God permits souls to go through these last trials in order to increase their merits. Souls that are strong and generous, in order that they may have a more glorious place in Heaven, have often had, at the end of their lives and in the moment of death, terrible combats with the angel of darkness.

"But they always come out victorious.

"God never allows a soul that has been devoted to Him

during life to perish at the last moment. Those souls who have loved the Blessed Virgin and invoked her all their lives receive from her many graces in their last struggles."

And because of that, every day we should set aside prayers for whoever in our family may be the next to pass on, so that when the day arrives, that person will have a "bank account" of prayers to draw from.

While those who have maintained Christian lives have little to worry about, there are a number of people who have reported negative death experiences. Instead of angels they see demons. This is precisely why we urge all Christians to call for Mary's special protection and the graces she has been allotted by Jesus.

The Virgin has a special mission against the serpent (*Genesis* 3:15).

She never fails. The more we've invoked the Virgin during life ("pray for us sinners now and at the hour of our death"), the stronger will we feel her presence.

Upon death she is there in a radiance just like what we hear from the greatest visionaries. She is full of light and beautiful—radiating like a jewel—because she's full of love.

When St. Clare saw Mary, the Virgin's diadem was brighter than the sun. Our Blessed Mother took St. Clare into her arms and gave her a holy kiss of peace. Clare's heart was filled with strength and happiness and the virgins who accompanied Mary spread a golden cover upon Clare's bed.

She is also an intermediary between the dead and living. At Medjugorje, Mary appeared on the day seer Jacov Colo's mother died and granted him the greatest consolation by informing him: *"Your mother is with me!"*

A similar thing occurred to seer Ivanka Elez, whose deceased mother was brought three times by Mary—and even hugged her daughter!

23

Chapter 8

One can only imagine the joy of seeing a departed parent.

This is all the beauty of life. This is the beauty of eternity.

The overwhelming majority of those who have encounter-ed death no longer have any fear of death. In fact, they look *forward* to it.

Heaven is an incredible place. We'll see that soon. But like I said, before we get to paradise, before we get to the place of Jesus and Mary, we must pass through judgment.

And that judgment is immediate. They say that upon death we're shown a playback of all the events in our lives. According to the Church, divine examination of the soul is instantaneous. God needs neither the testimony of witnesses nor the least discussion. The soul is instantly enlightened. In the words of one of the great theologians, Father Reginald Garrigou-Lagrange, "God knows by immediate intuition, and at the moment of separation the soul knows itself without medium. It is enlightened, decisively and inevitably, on all its merits and demerits. It sees its state without possibility of error, sees all that it has thought, desired, said, and done, both in good and in evil. It sees all the good it has omitted. Memory and conscience penetrate its entire moral and spiritual life, even to the minutest details."

Garrigou-Lagrange emphasized that upon death "the soul sees its entire past in a glance." The theologian quoted a cardinal who said in the first instant of separation from the body the soul commences to judge in the same manner as do pure spirits.

What's the judgment like?

It's not like entering a courtroom. There's no pompous judge in flowing black robe nor are there any lawyers. Instead there is Jesus or an angelic host who takes us through every minute of our lives and allows us to see ourselves from God's perspective.

Those who've had experiences with death say the incredible thing is that, as Garrigou-Lagrange wrote, the review of one's life occurs in what seems like a flash. In but a second, in but a moment of time, we see everything that ever happened and return to everywhere we've ever been.

We'll smell the aromas at grandma's house or see the objects tumbling out of our high-school lockers or hear the sounds of a long-past household as if we are there once again.

Upon death one's life is replayed and relived in a three-dimensional panorama. It's a bit like watching a movie. And it's full of surprise. Sometimes what seems great to us really counts as little and what's important to God seems trivial to us. Small things we don't think important may be treated with great significance while major earthly events may seem very small.

Those who are rich or in positions of power (see *Matthew* 19:24) are especially accountable.

The person undergoing the life review is *made to feel the emotions in every single person he or she has ever met and dealt with through life.* We're placed in the position of those we encountered. If we made someone feel happy, joyful, or comfortable, we feel those pleasant emotions. If we made someone feel anxious or hurt, if we insulted or slighted someone, we'll live that hurt ourselves.

Most incredibly, not only do we feel how we made everyone else feel but upon death we will also be made to see the surprising way that our treatment of one person may have affected others.

There can be a domino effect, and when we treat someone wrongly we contribute to an imbalance throughout the universe.

Births, deaths, marriage, joy, struggles, victories, defeats—all are replayed and so are our reactions. Some say they saw only the major events of their lives, but many seemed to relive every incident, from paying bills to household arguments.

"At the moment of death, God gives everyone the grace to see his whole life, to see what he has done, to recognize the results of his choices on earth," seer Marija Pavlovic of Medjugorje once told an interviewer. "And each person, when he sees himself in the divine light of reality, chooses for himself where he belongs. Every individual chooses for himself what he personally deserves for all eternity."

I've spoken to a few people who had this experience as part of a near-death encounter or as a grace given during prayer. One person, a television cameraman, described how he was shown his life while praying before the Blessed Sacrament. He was shocked at how each little violation of human and spiritual laws came back to him—how things he thought very minor, like exceeding the speed limit (which is a violation of civil authority), were taken into account. To what extent such seemingly insignificant violations matter in the afterlife are for others to debate, but the point is that all of life is full of significance. Nothing is meaningless to God. Especially important is how we've handled ourselves at home: whether as children we honored our parents and as parents whether we have given proper spiritual direction to our children.

At Medjugorje there was the account of a young Italian man who while praying before the Blessed Sacrament suddenly began to see the "film" of his life with great precision. According to one report, "Events re-emerged from his childhood and distant past, including completely forgotten scenes. From his more recent past, he saw things he had never considered in that way. It was as if he was reviewing all his life the way God Himself sees it. The Holy Spirit thus revealed to him the true meaning of his life and how much he was loved and cherished by God from the very beginning, even though he was not aware of it."

Events were replayed to show how even the bad was often employed by the Lord to create good results.

"God used the evil there had been in my life to bring me to Him, and I was amazed to see in what a marvelous way He had succeeded in leading me through evil as well as through good," this man told a nun. "I understood that in life, only love counts."

While that wasn't a death experience, those who report such encounters relate a similar life review and emphasize that it was not done to make them feel bad but rather to understand where their spirits stood in the eyes of God.

We realize in death, said Pope Gregory, how the "big" things in life are really not so big.

"He who is rapt in God can see without difficulty everything that is below God," he said in commenting on one man's death experience. "Therefore in that light that was shining before his exterior eyes, there was an inner light in his mind, which lifted his spirit to the heights and showed him how paltry were the things below."

The experience of reviewing a life can be like flipping

through a series of slides with incredible speed. "I saw my whole past life take place in many images, as though on a stage at some distance from me," said Swiss researcher Albert Heim, who himself had a brush with death.

A woman from Idaho recounted how in a flash she relived every thought and every word she ever spoke, as well as the effects of those words and deeds on everyone and everything around her.

It's as much a light of insight as a light of judgment. There's no harshness but simply an illumination that in a way allows the person to see where he had shortcomings and to judge himself.

More than a movie, it's a *reliving*.

But the judgment is firm.

During a visit to Louisiana I met a devout Catholic woman named Sondra Abrahams from Sulphur who said she "died" in 1970 after undergoing a hysterectomy.

"They gave me an anti-nausea drug that was brand new on the market," Sondra told me. "They gave me the medicine the day I was leaving to go home after the surgery. I felt odd that morning and the nurse thought it was just nervousness over going home because I had three very small children. My husband brought me home—my mother-in-law was there with the children. After he left and went back to work I went into the bedroom and started feeling funny in my throat and in my face. It felt like I was being paralyzed. My face was drawing back and I had no control over my mouth. My jaw was like locked together. And I told my mother-in-law to call my husband Kenneth immediately. I said, 'I think I'm having a stroke.'

"He rushed home and when he got home he took one look at me. Well, by then I was in great difficulty. I couldn't breathe and I could hardly talk. My throat was closing. He called the doctor and the doctor said to get me to the emergency room. I was having a reaction to the drug. We had a wild ride to the emergency room, and when we got there my husband carried me in. I can remember the table and even the direction it was facing, the doctor and on the other side the nurse. I can remember looking up at him. I was trying to breathe and trying to talk and I couldn't do either.

"And then he hit me in the chest. I guess I had gone into heart arrest and I remember looking down and seeing him hitting me on the chest. It's like I'm looking down at my own body. It was amazing. I'm looking down at him working on my body and hearing things that he was saying and seeing him throwing things and I remember thinking, 'That's me. That's me there.'

"And then all of a sudden I felt a pull, like something pulling me. And I was, like, up at the ceiling looking down and I was going through this dark tunnel. On each side of me there were little sparkly lights, like tiny firebugs all around me, and I looked up and remember seeing this light that was way down, this little bright light that, as I was getting to where I was going, was getting larger. I knew—I don't know how I knew, but I knew—I had to go to that light, that there was safety in the light. I went into the light and it was brilliant and the Light was Christ, and He looked just like He did when He ascended into Heaven. He wore the white tunic and He had His hands up. I saw the wounds. He just embraced me—and the love! I have never known that kind of love. I thought I knew what love was. Being a mother I love my children and grandchildren so much, but the love of Christ is so consuming, it's just unbelievable, beautiful. He spoke to me but it wasn't words. I could hear Him but I didn't see His lips moving. He was thinking from His mind to mine. He asked if I was satisfied with my life. I remember looking around. He pointed and whenever He did my whole life went from the time I was a little tiny child at the age of two on up to the birth of my three children and up to the present time. It was just like a movie, seeing my life. I could see everything I had ever done wrong—He showed that to me—and everyone I could have helped and I didn't! And oh gosh, there were a lot of people I could have helped that I didn't. I felt His sorrow that I had turned my back on them."

Chapter 9

In the love of Christ is the desire that we too love. More than anything, we're judged on the size of our hearts. We're judged on that time we stopped to let a pedestrian cross a street or did a chore normally assigned to someone else or helped with the groceries when it really wasn't our job. All these "little" things can have resounding consequences.

"At the evening of death, we shall be judged on our love," emphasizes the *Catechism*.

We're judged on our love as well as how much we've followed the Commandments. Throughout the New Testament are guidelines for how we should act in any situation of life and following the Bible to the letter, following the teachings of Our Savior, is the safest way of making sure that the life review, when it comes, is favorable.

Aside from the major sins, aside from avoiding adultery and hatred, theft and murder, aside from taking care to honor our parents and tending to personal morals, we must be careful not to be jealous when we should be happy for someone or covetous when we should wish someone the best or impatient when we are being tested for our long-suffering.

Every minute of life is a test and every single one of those minutes will come flooding back to us.

We will be evaluated both on the good works we have done and how much we have loved and served God.

Every thought will be there. Every emotion is on record. And in one simple glance Christ knows exactly where we stand and where we need to go. It's displayed in our spirits. It's whiteness and darkness.

The judgment is described not as a systematic process but rather something that occurs automatically. God gives us His Light and with that light we see ourselves as He sees us. We then go to where we belong. The soul gravitates. Dark goes to dark, white goes to white, with any number of stages in-between. A soul in need of purification would no sooner head for Heaven than would a person in faded jeans and muddy shoes attend an elegant wedding.

"The soul sees how God judged," Father Garrigou-Lagrange had said, "and conscience makes this judgment definitive."

Some believe that upon death all souls, no matter where they're going, get a glimpse of God and Heaven. It's a debatable matter and we can't become too attached to any one idea, but you get the point: upon death we realize once and for all that God exists and that everything we do is important, especially how much we love God and our fellow humans. Those with the stain of sin now understand the serious nature of Catholic doctrine and why it's so strict: it aims at sending Catholics to Heaven and at avoiding Hell.

While New Agers and secular humanists try to put a "don't-worry-about-anything" spin on death experiences, and while in most cases the process of death has very pleasant components, that's not to say there is nothing to be concerned about. That's not to say there's no purification after the pleasant departure. It's certainly not to deny the awful reality of eternal fire for those who deny and curse God.

Incredible as it may seem, there are those who are so full of pride and hatred that even at the very last moment, even when they glimpse eternity, they refuse to budge from their resentment of the Lord. Such resentment and unrepentance, such rejection of final grace, is a sin against the Holy Spirit. And as it says in *Mark* 3:29, "whoever blasphemes against the Holy Spirit will never be forgiven. He carries the guilt of his sin without end."

Our *Catechism* repeats that truth and tells us that God predestines no one for Hell.

For that to happen, there must be a willful turning away from God (a mortal sin) and persistence in it until the end.

When we die our spirits meld into love or hate.

Heaven is love.

Hatred is Hell.

The ticket to eternal fire is thus to be full of hate, which is rejection of God. Where God sends love, Hell sends malice. When we have malice, when we hate or lack charity, we're rejecting our Creator and in league with the devil.

Satan is pride and pride is the source of most evil. It's the source of everything from hate to materialism. "All vices have one root in common, namely, the disordered love of self, opposed to the love of good, and especially of the sovereign good which is God," said Father Garrigou-Lagrange. "This evil root tends to sink itself ever more deeply into the will, and from this root there is born an evil tree. The trunk of this tree is egoism, of which the central and principal branch, the continuation of the trunk, is pride, of which the lateral branches are the concupiscence (lust) of the flesh and the concupiscence of the eyes. The branches of this wicked tree have numerous sub-branches which are called capital sins."

The more pride we have, the less love we have. That leads to hate and think about it: to hate is to have strong ill will for somebody. When you hate or are jealous you are wishing bad things on someone. Wishing bad things is a curse; you're placing a curse on the person. It reminds us of witchcraft. And as with a witch, the hatred, the inner malice, externalizes and registers in our features. It makes us *ugly*. After death the soul takes on the appearance of its feelings and so just as love brings beauty, so does hate bring a haggish, ugly appearance. In the afterlife our emotions are literally written on our features. Those who are arrogant look disgusting and those with hatred and beastly lusts look like animals.

I wouldn't want to detail some of the beastly descriptions; they're revolting. They remind us of growling, loathsome animals with matted fur.

During the famous apparitions at Fatima, Sister Lucia dos Santos said she was shown a vision of "a great sea of fire which seemed to be under the earth. Plunged in this fire were demons and souls in human form, like transparent burning embers, all blackened or burnished bronze, floating about in the conflagration, now raised into the air by the flames that issued from within themselves together with great clouds of smoke, now falling back on every side like sparks in a huge fire, without weight or equilibrium, and amid shrieks and groans of pain and despair, which horrified us and made us tremble with fear. The demons could be distinguished by their terrifying and repellent likeness to frightful and unknown animals, all black and transparent."

One day while tending sheep at a place called Pedreira, little Francisco Marto saw "one of those huge beasts that we saw in Hell. He was right here breathing out flames!"

At Medjugorje, Marija has described Hell as "a large space with a big sea of fire in the middle. There are many people there. I particularly noticed a beautiful young girl. But when she came near the fire, she was no longer beautiful. She came out of the fire like an animal; she was no longer human."

I also knew an alleged visionary who saw Hell as a muddy

swamp with islands and disfigured humans trudging through the mud toward a terribly ugly woman who seemed to be their boss on a central island.

Chapter 10

Other depictions are so distasteful I choose not to present them. At Medjugorje the visionaries have explained that for those whose lives have been full of sin, Hell is the only place they would fit in. Through free will, through sin against God, they have chosen it for themselves. Hell exists for those who select it out of their own final rejection of God. Atheists are thus at special risk—greater risk, perhaps, than even a murderer who repents before death and at least acknowledges the Lord. Atheism is denying God His very role and constitutes an incredible degree of arrogance and ingratitude.

To reject God is to reject Heaven. It's a sin against the Holy Spirit. And it is not uncommon. *"Today many persons go to Hell,"* warned the Virgin of Medjugorje. *"God allows His children to suffer in Hell due to the fact that they have committed grave, unpardonable sins. Those who are in Hell no longer have a chance to know a better lot."*

A Christian doctor named Maurice Rawlings has written about a number of people who've had frightening glimpses of Hell. He believes many more have such experiences but quickly forget them. Dr. Rawlings cites patients who saw Hell as slimy earth that was red and hot and full of devils that mocked each other. One person saw a huge giant with a grotesque face.

Others have actually seen a lake of brimstone. There are those who come out of their death encounters sweating, trembling, and with grotesque grimaces indicating sheer horror.

Recently, I was asked if Hell could really be forever. I was asked if the souls might not be saved from Hell at the last judgment.

I can't speak for the Church when it comes to the last judgment but I can say that both the Bible and *Catechism* speak of Hell as a fire that can never be quenched and as "everlasting" and "eternal" (for example: see *Matthew* 25:41 and *Mark* 9:43).

When Our Blessed Mother was asked how a merciful God could allow Hell, she replied, *"Men who go to Hell no longer want to receive any benefit from God. They do not repent nor do they cease to revolt and to blaspheme. They make up their minds to live in Hell and do not contemplate leaving."*

Our Lord once told St. Therese, "My daughter, no one is lost without knowing it."

And she added at Medjugorje, *"Those who say, 'I do not believe in God,' how difficult it will be for them when they will approach the Throne of God and hear the voice: 'Enter into Hell.'"*

Writing in a book called *Le Christ au Monde*, Abbe F. Chatel commented, "All the truths taught to us by the Church concerning Hell are terrible; but it is a question of grave offenses against the Most High and very holy majesty of God, of crushing underfoot the Blood of Jesus Christ, of profaning the temple of the Holy Spirit and to drive Him out of us unworthily, abusing His grace, preferring the creature to God, responding to all of His goodness to us by blasphemy and ingratitude, and failing to fulfill the purpose for which our souls have been created."

The reason Jesus spoke so much of Hell, said Thomas Aquinas, was that to the sinner talk of Hell is more compelling than talk of Heaven.

Those who've had death experiences sometimes relate their brush with demons in a horrid netherworld.

"They began clawing at me and biting at me," said a former art professor who had one such encounter. "And just as I'd get one off, it seemed as though five more would be back on me, clawing and pushing. I had the sense that there were innumerable numbers of people clawing at me, working to make me as miserable as possible. It was essentially an atmosphere of darkness, fear, pain, and utter loneliness."

The teacher was brought back to life and given a second chance after invoking God. The same happened to an unbelieving young person who was sarcastic toward religion and made fun of its truths. He had the horrifying experience of going into a coma and being buried before coming back to life and knocking on the coffin so loud that a gravedigger heard him. "When I regained consciousness in the grave and recognized the frightful reality of my burial, when after having uttered shrieks, I endeavored to break my coffin, and struck my forehead against the boards, I saw that all was useless," he recounted. "Death appeared to me with all its horrors; it was less bodily than the eternal death that frightened me. I saw I was going to be damned."

If all the stars of Heaven were licks of fire, said another who was sent to Hell, "they could not express what torments I endure!"

Yet we hear little about this. Many don't want to publicize it. It seems "unpleasant." But we must all know the truth and help those we know who may be headed there.

A famous researcher said less than one percent of those who were near death reported Hell during their death experiences but the proportion would be higher, argues Dr. Rawlings, except for the fact that many who have the hellish experience seem to erase it from their minds immediately after the horrible encounter.

Another researcher tallied five out of 40 interviewees, or 13 percent, as having negative or Hell experiences.

Hell is described as like falling into a dark bottomless pit instead of traveling to the light.

It can be either unbearably hot or unbearably cold.

And often the odor of decay is associated with it.

"The entrance, I thought, resembled a very long, narrow passage, like a furnace, very low, dark, and closely confined," wrote St. Teresa of Avila, who had a mystical vision of the netherworld. "The ground seemed to be full of water which looked like filthy, evil-smelling mud, and in it were many wicked-looking reptiles. At the end there was a hollow place scooped out of a wall, like a cupboard."

There's a terrible noise in Hell, a constant inhuman wailing that recalls what Christ said about an "outer darkness" where there would be "wailing" as well as the "gnashing of teeth" (*Matthew* 8:12 KJV).

Dr. Rawlings has recorded cases in which those who "died" have seen flames like an oil fire.

"The heat is dry, a dehydrating type," he wrote. "Your eyeballs are so dry they feel like red-hot coals in their sockets."

As another has recounted, "As far as my eyes could see it was just the same. A lake of fire and brimstone."

This is in keeping with *Revelation* 21:8, which says that "the cowards and traitors to the faith, the depraved and murderers, the fornicators and sorcerers, the idol-worshipers and deceivers and every sort" find their lot in "the fiery pool of burning sulphur." Jesus Himself described a rich man who indulged himself shamelessly while ignoring the poor and ended up tormented in flames that were separated from Heaven by a "great abyss" (*Luke* 16:25).

In Itatina, Peru, a servant woman who died around 1500 allegedly materialized to three people and said, "Know that I am damned and that I suffer horribly because I had declared in Confession only my slightest faults, accusing myself, for example, of having spoken too much, of having been angry and so forth, while I hid my gravest sins. God orders me to give you this warning so that you may give it to others."

Chapter 11

To think that such torment lasts forever, to think that these souls are deprived God's Presence for eternity, is an awesome thought. Let's not get too wrapped up in the negative but we must know that Hell does exist and that some people find themselves there.

St. Teresa described Hell as the "blackest darkness." The physical pains are never-ceasing and intolerable. There is no hope. There is no consolation. It is as if the soul is tearing itself to pieces.

"The fact is that I cannot find words to describe that interior fire and that despair, which is greater than the most grievous tortures and pains," said St. Teresa, who added that Hell is "an oppression, a suffocation and an affliction so deeply felt, and accompanied by such hopeless and distressing misery, that I cannot too forcibly describe it."

The demons are for those who have invited or worshipped demons. The demons are those who, like Satan, have rebelled against God. The demons are those who have consciously rejected Heaven. I think especially of satanists who conspire to challenge the Lord's authority and people who put no value on human life.

Those who seek to dispel God, to undermine belief in Him,

and to challenge His right as Creator—especially those who tinker with the very stuff of life itself—are in the greatest danger. I cringe when I think that scientists even now are trying to clone humans!

I'm not God and I can't judge everything that brings condemnation but Christ described those who would be damned as *"all who draw others to apostasy and all evildoers."* Our *Catechism* tells us that "those who die in a state of mortal sin descend into Hell," where the greatest suffering is not the mud or the demons or the truly blazing fire but complete separation from the vision of God.

There is no limiting God's mercy. There are opportunities for repentance right to the last breath. But anyone who deliberately refuses to accept that mercy rejects God's salvation. Mortal sin is specified in the Bible, especially in the Ten Commandments, and is a deliberate choice.

Unintentional ignorance diminishes the serious nature of the sin but every person is born with moral intuition—with a built-in code of what is good and what is wrong, no matter what his or her religious orientation—and so we are all subject to God's judgment.

That doesn't mean we can judge others. We do not have the information to judge. There are many factors that only God can evaluate. He evaluates the demons people are born with, the rearing in school, the religious education, the family life, the personality, the innermost struggles, and a person's spiritual opportunities before rendering His unchallengeable verdict.

Those who have had access to much information are more answerable than those who were raised in ignorance.

I know a priest, Father Steven Scheier, who broke his neck in a car accident. It was during 1988. His car crashed head-on with a pickup truck, and half his scalp was torn off. He was given but a 15 percent chance of survival.

Later he recalled that at one point he'd undergone a life review and due to his sinfulness and falsity as a priest was headed for Hell.

It was then a conversation took place.

"Son, will you please spare his life and his eternal soul?" said a female he heard.

"Mother, he has been a priest for 12 years for himself and not for me," said Christ. "Let him reap the punishment he deserves."

"But Son, if we give him special graces and strength (we can) then see if he bears fruit. If not, Your will be done."

"Mother, he's yours," the priest heard before recovering.

Chapter 12

That's the mercy of Christ.

There is also the mercy of Purgatory.

For most of us that's the first eternal stop.

At Medjugorje the Virgin said that many go to Hell, a small number go directly to Heaven, and that the majority of people go to Purgatory. It's the huge area between Heaven and Hell. It's the place where everything from minor faults to serious sin are purged. It's a gray area just as there are gray areas in all aspects of existence.

But in the case of Purgatory it's gray *literally*. Although it too has fire, especially at its lowest depth (which borders Hell), for the most part Purgatory is described as a sort of dreary and foggy area. You could call it "the gray zone." It has been a concept in the Church since the earliest days and has been formally accepted since the Middle Ages. The official recognition of Purgatory can be found in a letter by Pope Innocent IV in 1254 and at the Second Council of Lyon soon after (then later at the Council of Trent). Although Protestants have erased it, Purgatory was even accepted by their founder, Martin Luther. "All who die in God's grace and friendship, but still imperfectly purified, are indeed assured of their eternal salvation," says the *Catechism*. "But after death they undergo purification, so as to achieve the holiness necessary to enter the joy of Heaven."

When we comprehend that only perfect purity leads to God's Presence we realize that the vast majority of people, Christian or non-Christian, need purification—including those who, in their pride, believe they merit Heaven. Unless you're flawless, unless you have purged all your imperfections here on earth (often through suffering) and are in perfect union with God, you are headed for a stint, however brief, in Purgatory.

There God takes the souls He loves and breaks down all its pretenses.

You're purified like precious metal.

When the defects are gone, when the soul is broken down, when the selfishness is removed, the Lord then reforms the soul and gives it the pure apparel necessary to enter the wedding.

Such notions are not Catholic fantasy. Among other places you can find allusions to Purgatory in the Bible. In *II Maccabees* 12:42-46 it relates how a man named Judas and his army gathered up the dead, prayed for them, and even provided for sacrifice. Atonement was made "that they might be freed from this sin." Another translation of this text clearly states that "it is a holy and wholesome thought to pray for the dead to be loosed from their sins." It says that what these ancients did for the slain was "pray for them in death."

If that's not clear enough, there's also *2 Timothy* 1:16-18 where Paul speaks of his departed friend Onesiphorus and says, "When he stands before the Lord on the great Day, may the Lord grant him mercy" (which makes sense only if this deceased man can be helped by prayer), and *1 Samuel* 31:13 where it's implied that the residents of Jabesh fasted for Saul and his sons after disposing of their remains—again indicating Purgatory. There is written evidence from as long ago as A.D.

211 that Christians prayed and sacrificed for the deceased (see the writings of Tertullian, who said such sacrifices were made on the birthdays and anniversaries of the dead), and there's no doubt ancient Jews prayed for those in the afterlife. It was an established part of synagogue ritual.

Unfortunately many Protestants have deleted *Maccabees* from the Bible but that doesn't change the truth. Purgatory exists and most of us face its purification. When we sin our souls are tainted. There's darkness. There's spiritual grit. That must be removed and the extent and duration of cleansing obviously depends on the depth and breadth of contamination.

"In Purgatory there are different levels," explained Mary at Medjugorje. *"The lowest is close to Hell and the highest gradually draws near Heaven."*

This is in accord with St. Augustine, who said the same fire that tortures the damned "purifies the elect."

Chapter 13

How does God determine if we go to Purgatory and at what level?

Humans are unable to judge where anyone will go. God's judgments are different from those of the world. He takes into account infinite factors. He takes into account things we would never know or even think of. He takes into account hidden burdens as well as obvious factors like character and temperament. He takes into account the wisdom we're raised with. He takes into account our genetic baggage. Only He knows how much He must purify us because only He knows the secret recesses of a soul.

This much we can surmise: at the lowest reaches of Purgatory, in the bowels of the earth, are those who have very seriously offended God and would have gone to Hell but for last-minute mercy, last-minute repentance, last-minute reprieve. At the low level are probably murderers, occultists, abortionists, rapists, child molesters, thieves, tyrants, sadists, and those involved in various criminal activities.

A safe bet is that you'd also find repentant adulterers, sodomists, and idolaters.

No matter the sin, if a person repents he is saved from the

eternal fire and instead finds his way to the fire of Purgatory.

But what a fire it is! It's always described as hotter than any earthly fire. There, an hour of torment is more terrible than an entire lifetime of suffering on earth. I've seen descriptions of souls who are in a covered well full of fantastic heat and there are accounts of departed souls who've returned as apparitions and done such things as leave a burnt hand mark on a wood door as if with a red-hot iron. When Drythelm saw the valley there was "all fire on one side, all ice and snow on the other; on the one hand braziers and caldrons of flame, on the other the most intense cold and the blast of a glacial wind. This mysterious valley was filled with innumerable souls, which, tossed as by a furious tempest, threw themselves from one side to the other. When they could no longer endure the violence of the fire, they sought relief amidst the ice and snow; but finding only a new torture, they cast themselves again into the midst of the flames."

It may surprise you that there's fire in Purgatory but such is mentioned by many mystics. God purifies with His fire, and the lowest levels of Purgatory are similar to Hell. The soul may even have a disfigured or beastly quality but unlike Hell those who are at any level of Purgatory bear the consolation of knowing their souls are saved and that one day they'll be allowed into Heaven. No matter the intensity of their suffering (and it is *intense*) there is the consoling realization that God exists and that one day they will be in His Presence.

The sentences God metes out rely on innumerable factors but one might surmise that lowest Purgatory also has its share of liars, conmen, philanderers, false prophets, fortunetellers, money-grabbers, and those who have repented but not yet expiated for their misdeeds. Just as we can never judge the destination of a particular soul, neither can we take sin and neatly categorize it. It's not possible to give a roadmap of where sin will lead in the afterlife. It depends on God. It depends on what we have accumulated and what we have cleared through Confession.

The best I can do is present the comments of those who claim to have seen Purgatory.

One woman who tried to commit suicide in 1991 recalled a death experience in which she landed on a shadowy plane with black mist swirling around her.

The mist formed a barrier that kept her prisoner and it was like space but without a single glimmering star.

What comes to mind again is the "outer darkness" referred to by Christ in *Matthew* 8:12, for the foglike mist had mass— "it seemed to be formed of molecules of intense darkness"— and the woman, Angie Fenimore, saw men and women of all ages but no children.

The people were squatting or wandering around and there seemed to be a darkness that flowed from deep within them. They were crippled by it. They were so absorbed with it, so caught up in their own woe, that they didn't want to participate in mental or emotional exchange.

Some wore dirty white robes. Others were deeply soiled. They were there to admit and understand the mistakes in their lives and it was a place, she said, of stifling torment "that awaited me for taking my own life."

From the Soviet Union came a similar account of a man whose sin was atheism. Like suicide, atheism robs God of His role as Creator and landed the man, a medical doctor named George Rodonaia, in a very frightening place when he "died" in 1976 after being hit by a car.

Dr. Rodonaia (now a Christian minister in the U.S.) was dead for hours, until a pathologist began to cut his abdomen during an autopsy!

Like Angie he had found himself in a realm of total darkness. The gloom was absolute, "darker than any dark, blacker than any black," and he was both shocked and horrified.

He was shocked that he existed without a body and horrified at the void in which he found himself.

It was only when he turned from his negativity that the Light of God broke that awful darkness.

St. Catherine of Genoa informed us that "souls in a state of purification are tormented to the point that words cannot describe, nor can any intelligence give even the slightest idea unless God manifests this through a special grace."

While certain purgatories are not so bad, at the low places, at the deep levels, it's very trying. In 1873 a holy nun identified only as Sister M. de L.C. in a French convent began to hear prolonged sighs beside her. The strange noises from an invisible presence went on and came nearer. In February of 1874, after much prayer and many Communions, the presence finally identified itself to Sister M as the spirit of a second nun we'll call Sister O who had also been at the convent but who died several years before and was now in Purgatory.

"Great sinners who were indifferent towards God, and religious who were not what they should have been, are in the lowest stage of Purgatory," revealed Sister O. "While they are there, the prayers offered up for them are not applied to them. Because they have ignored God during their lives, He now in His turn leaves them abandoned in order that they may repair their neglectful and worthless lives. While on earth one truly cannot picture or imagine what God really is, but we in Purgatory know and understand Him for what He is, because our souls are freed from all ties that fettered them and prevented them from realizing the holiness and majesty of God, and His great mercy. We are martyrs, consumed as it were by love. An irresistible force draws us towards God Who is our center, but at the same time another force thrusts us back to our place of expiation.

"We are in a state of being unable to satisfy our longings. Oh, what a suffering that is, but we desire it and there is no murmuring against God here. We desire only what God wants. You on earth, however, cannot possibly understand what we have to endure. I am much relieved as I am no longer in the fire. I have now only the insatiable desire to see God, a suffering cruel enough indeed, but I feel that the end of my exile is at hand and that I am soon to leave this place where I long for God with all my heart.

"I can tell you about the different degrees of Purgatory because I have passed through them. In the great Purgatory there are several stages. In the lowest and most painful, like a temporary Hell, are the sinners who have committed terrible crimes during life and whose death surprised them in that state. It was almost a miracle that they were saved, and often by prayers of holy parents or other pious persons. Sometimes they did not even have time to confess their sins and the world thought them lost, but God, Whose mercy is infinite, gave them at the moment of death the contrition necessary for their salvation on account of one or more good actions which they performed during life. For such souls, Purgatory is terrible. It is real Hell, with this difference, that in Hell they curse God, whereas we bless Him and thank Him for having saved us.

"Next to these come the souls, who though they did not commit great crimes like the others, were indifferent to God. They did not fulfill their Easter duties and were also converted at the point of death. Perhaps they were unable to receive Holy Communion. They are in Purgatory for the long years of indifference. They suffer unheard of pains and are abandoned either without prayers or if they are said for them, they are not allowed to profit by them.

"In the second Purgatory are the souls of those who died with venial sins not fully expiated before death, or with mortal sins that have been forgiven but for which they have not made entire satisfaction to the Divine Justice. In this part of Purgatory, there are also different degrees according to the merits of each soul.

"Lastly, there is the Purgatory of desire which is called the Threshold. Very few escape this. To avoid it altogether, one must ardently desire Heaven and the Vision of God. That is rare, rarer than people think, because even pious people are afraid of God and have not, therefore, sufficiently strong desire of going to Heaven. This Purgatory has its very painful martyrdom like the others. The deprivation of the sight of our loving Jesus adds to the intense suffering. It is a continuous martyrdom. It makes me suffer more than does the fire of Purgatory. It is so beautiful in Heaven. There is a great distance between Purgatory and Heaven. We are privileged at times to catch glimpses of the joys of the blessed in paradise, but it is almost a punishment. It makes us yearn to see God. In Heaven it is pure delight; in Purgatory, profound darkness. Oh, how I desire to go to Heaven! What a martyrdom we suffer once we have seen God!"

Chapter 14

For several years there was communication from the deceased nun. While the Church is very cautious with such revelation and where the average person is warned about communicating with the dead, it was clearly a special case designed by Heaven and the revelations were approved by noted theologians like Canon Dubosq, *promotor fidei* of St. Therese the Little Flower and granted an imprimatur by Cardinal Lawrence Shehan of Baltimore. (See Notes for how to obtain them.) It may be the most valuable document I've read on Purgatory.

Hardly any souls love God as they should, warned Sister O, and it is only the souls who perfectly conform to His Will who immediately receive their reward without passing through Purgatory. There has to be self-control. There has to be perfect spiritual balance. Life must be lived with pure, heroic love. Life must be lived for Jesus and only Jesus. No suffering is too much. "What are the few moments we have to pass on earth compared to eternity?" asked Sister O in these revelations. "At the very hour of death, you will not find that you have done too much. Be very generous, do not listen to yourself but always look at the goal to which Jesus calls you. That is, sanctity, pure love. Then go forward and never look back. Great crosses,

crosses that often break the heart, so to say, are the portion of God's own friends. Oh, how little people on earth understand what a degree of detachment Jesus demands of a soul whom He wishes to make all His own. People think they love and will soon become saints because they feel a little more sensible devotion than usual, but all these natural devotions are as nothing. A soul must rise up and detach itself from its self-love, its passions. The Holy Eucharist must be as a magnet for you, drawing you always more and more powerfully. This sacrament must be the main object of your life.

"Your whole heart and soul must be submerged in Him," cautioned Sister O, "so that you do nothing except what is His pleasure. Rise above earthly things and your surroundings to lose yourself entirely in His Will," added the nun, to use a composite quote.

Souls in Purgatory communicate with each other when God permits it but do not know exactly when they will be released. In the meantime, except for the deepest levels, the Blessed Mother occasionally consoles them. On feast days her presence lights up Purgatory with its great splendor; the Virgin once told St. Bridget that she is the queen of those in purgatorial suffering and that she prays to lessen those sufferings. At her very presence the dark or grayness is lit with a light that falls with particular favor upon those who wore the Scapular and had a special devotion to her Immaculate Heart. Indeed Mary promised that those wearing a Scapular and adhering closely to the teachings of Jesus will be freed by her the first Saturday after their deaths.

Sister O begged prayers for those in Purgatory and like others said there were many souls who were abandoned with no one to pray for them. "No one can have a real understanding of the sufferings in Purgatory," she said. "No one thinks of them in the world. Even religious communities forget that they should pray for the poor souls and that they should inspire their pupils with this devotion."

As seer Mirjana Soldo of Medjugorje once said, many who die are abandoned by their loved ones and cannot help themselves in Purgatory. They are totally dependent on the prayer and sacrifice of others to make restitution.

The average stay in Purgatory, said Sister O, was what on earth would be comparable to perhaps 30 or 40 years.

"I tell you in terms of earthly calculations because here it is quite different," she explained. "Oh, if people only knew and understood what Purgatory is and what it means to know that we are here through our own fault. I have been here eight years and it seems to me like ten thousand."

Sister O was suffering because she abused graces during her life and caused her Mother Superior as well as others to suffer. She was lax in her life vocation.

A cloistered nun has a different set of both opportunities and standards.

"Alas," she said, "if you knew what the heat of Purgatory is compared to yours! A little prayer does much good. It is like a glass of water given to a thirsty person."

Chapter 15

The point is that God wants us to love Him for His own sake. He wants us to love Him with pure intention. It's a chief test of life and an important determinant on where we'll spend our Purgatory. God wants true friends with deep devotion. The key is to suffer well on earth—to accept the trials during life—and seek only to please God: to seek Him only.

"You must become indifferent to everything except what is for God," urged Sister O. "Thus you will reach the height of perfection to which Jesus calls you. Oh, if only we were allowed to come back to earth, after knowing what God really is, what a different life we would lead!

"Sacrifice and immolate yourself for Him," she urged. "You can never do enough for Him. God wishes you to concern yourself with Him alone, with His love and with the accomplishment of His holy will."

Such devotion greatly lessens Purgatory and allows the devout to escape many unpleasant circumstances in the afterlife. For there are endless situations. There are endless environments. And there are many torments. Those who were involved in sexual impurity may now find themselves in a

56

chamber full of filth. They might find themselves in a pestilential dungeon, the sight of which would produce nausea. The ambitious and proud might find themselves in frightful obscurity while those who lied may find a constant burning of their tongues.

For shepherds of the Church, Purgatory can be especially rigorous because they've been given special grace and have a greater crown awaiting them. And while it may not be the lowest level, there is obviously heat at a number of purgatories. As St. Margaret Mary Alacoque, the seer of the Sacred Heart, recounted: "On one occasion when I was praying before the Blessed Sacrament on the Feast of Corpus Christi, a person suddenly appeared before me all enveloped in flames, the heat of which penetrated me so powerfully that I believed myself to be burning as well. The pitiable condition in which I beheld him caused me to shed an abundance of tears. He told me that he was that Benedictine monk to whom I once went to Confession, and who ordered me to go to Holy Communion, and that as a reward for this, God had allowed him to have recourse to me that he might obtain some alleviation in his sufferings. He asked me to apply to his soul all I should do and suffer for three months, which I promised with the consent of my superiors. He then went on to say that the cause of his suffering was his preferring his own interests to the glory of God, through too great attachment to his own reputation; secondly, a want of charity towards his brethren; and finally, too natural an affection for creatures, many proofs of which he had manifested in his spiritual dealings with them, thereby greatly displeasing God."

For three months Margaret Mary suffered unbearably for that soul. It wasn't a long purgatory but certainly a hot and intense one.

Some souls are placed at deeper levels as an act of mercy,

so that their purgatories are shortened.

I don't know what level this soul was at but St. Margaret said "it would be difficult for me to express what I had to suffer during those three months. For he never left me, and on the side on which he stood, I seemed to be all on fire; this caused me such intense suffering that my tears and groans were continual."

Chapter 16

Most don't return to tell about Purgatory but we can be relatively sure that those in both the lower and middle reaches suffer in many ways. I wish I could lighten it. I can't. The truth is the truth and it should set us free. Those who in reading such accounts get "scared" need to evaluate what it is that scares them. All of us should realize we have time to avoid such suffering. It's that word penance or "expiation." If we expiate on earth we avoid unpleasant purgatories. If not, there are the lower or middle levels where souls are saved but must be purged. There's a price to pay. Confession is crucial. It saves our souls. It says we're sorry. We get absolution. But we must complete it through expiation. Simply saying we're sorry doesn't mean we go directly to Heaven. Only a spotless soul is allowed to stand immediately in the Presence of God and during an entire lifetime you don't meet many souls that are immaculate!

Most head for purgation and much of the cleansing takes place, if not at the lowest levels, at middle places that are dreary and lonely. You don't hear much about Purgatory in near-death stories either because the person blots it out, remembering only the pleasant aspects, or most likely because those who return are drawn back to the body before this detention is pronounced.

As we move up in Purgatory there may be less overt suffering, there may be less heat and less cold, but there is loneliness. One gets the impression of solitary souls pining for their loved ones. That seems the definition of Purgatory. People are lonesome for God. They're lonesome for the loved ones who greeted them upon death and now await them in Heaven. "They are so lonely that it is almost sickening to remember," said Vicka, the visionary from Medjugorje. They're lonesome because according to Sister O the average stay in Purgatory is several decades (but can range from a few moments—usually for holy priests—to centuries for hardened criminals). She said, "In Purgatory, as in Heaven, religious and those of the same family are not always together. Souls do not all merit the same punishment or the same reward. Still in Purgatory we do recognize others and if God permits it we may communicate with one another. Thoughts of earth can be made known here, but there is not much in all that, because I have already told you that the souls in Purgatory know those persons who interest themselves in their behalf on earth. About the time of our release we know nothing. If we only knew when the end of our sufferings would come it would be an intense relief, a joy for us, but no, it is not so. We know well that our sufferings decrease and our union with God becomes closer, but what day (that is according to earthly calculations, because here there are no days) we shall be united to God, of that we know nothing; it is a secret."

There is the sense that most people are at the middle levels of the Great Purgatory.

How many sublevels are there?

The number is probably vast, perhaps infinite.

"In the second Purgatory are the souls of those who died with venial sins not fully expiated before death, or with mortal sins that have been forgiven but for which they have not made entire satisfaction to the divine justice," commented Sister O. "In this part of Purgatory, there are also different degrees according to the merits of each soul."

It's the place where heat and darkness, where black, turn to gray. Vicka described it as a big space with thick fog, the people moaning, weeping, or trembling. Marija has said it is a "very misty" place with "a lot of voices begging for our prayers." They seem immersed in deep clouds and they are often souls who didn't pray enough or believe enough in God.

It's a place for those of doubt.

Now that they've seen God they're full of regret and harbor that intense longing to be close to Him.

No soul would want to leave Purgatory and come back to earth—they have a knowledge of God that is infinitely greater than ours and never again would they want to spend time in the spiritual blindness of earth—but their suffering is very lonely and they desperately need our prayers.

"There are many souls in Purgatory," said the Virgin at Medjugorje. *"There are also persons who have been consecrated to God—some priests, some religious. Pray for their intentions, at least the* Lord's Prayer *the* Hail Mary *and the* Glory Be *seven times each, and the* Creed. *I recommend it to you. There is a large number of souls in Purgatory for a long time because no one prays for them."*

Most powerful for such souls is the Mass as well as the Way of the Cross and Rosary. The Mass is the power of Jesus on the Cross and can atone for any sinner. All of us are part of God's design and lives lived without love for God must be atoned for by suffering. Lives that focus on the body, that live for the body instead of the spirit, and that seek to avoid all suffering are headed for a long purgatory while those who are reverent during life, especially through the Eucharist—those who glorify God and do His will—escape such punishment.

The more we detach ourselves from worldly things, the

more we mortify ourselves, the more we distance ourselves from the passions of flesh, the closer we grow to Christ and the farther we are from the Great Purgatory.

We don't *have* to go there. We have the chance now, right now, while on earth, to escape it. The key is in the Ten Commandments and the key is also in avoiding the capital sins of pride, lust, greed, sloth, envy, anger, and gluttony.

Many are those who don't realize they're sinning when they commit masturbation or fornication (which means sex before marriage) and many are those who, because society currently condones it, don't think it's a big deal to commit serious sins like adultery and homosexuality.

No matter what our corrupt society tries to tell us, we must be on special guard against sins of the flesh, and that includes all forms of impurity.

I can't say what gets a soul into certain parts of Purgatory but we all know we must be on special guard against hateful, jealous, or uncharitable thoughts. We must be very careful in speaking about others. The spirit of criticality is wrong, not to mention slander, which is a form of theft because it "steals" a person's reputation.

We must be patient and kind. We must purge all hate and grow in love no matter the circumstances. We must try to get to the point where nothing causes us upset or irritation. And we must also be careful on how we use God's name. It should never be used in exasperation. It should never be used in vain. We should kneel each time we're in remembrance of Christ and His Name should be used only with the utmost reverence, making sure we keep Sunday holy.

Chapter 17

And we should show gratitude. We should thank God for everything in life. We thank Him for the easy times and thank Him for the trials, which are His way of caressing and purging us. When we suffer well on earth it erases entire decades of Purgatory.

Asked how a person can do Purgatory on earth, Padre Pio once remarked, "By accepting everything from God's hands. By offering everything up to Him with love and thanksgiving so as to enable us to pass from our deathbed to paradise."

The bottom line: Every minute on earth is an opportunity to merit Heaven and escape Purgatory. In the afterlife we can no longer sin because we no longer have free will. The test is over. Now the wrong decisions must be atoned for and that can take seconds, minutes, days, months, or years. According to writer Jan Connell, the seer Marija was told that a person remains in Purgatory "until someone else among the people still on earth corrects, through God's graciousness, all the deliberate violations that soul has caused to God's loving plan for the universe and His beloved children who interacted, in His plan, with that soul. Marija has said that the Blessed Mother told her one hour in Purgatory is more painful than the longest, hardest life on earth."

As I mentioned, some say there are terms in Purgatory that last centuries. At Fatima the children were told of one soul who would be in Purgatory until the end of the world.

Others say there are souls—especially loving and devout souls—who fly right through and are with God the day they die.

This is especially true of devout nuns and priests, who may pass through Purgatory so fast they hardly catch a glimpse of it.

The key is expiation and that comes through earthly trials. On earth we'll never understand the mystery of suffering, but it corrects, it purifies. I'm not saying all suffering is necessary. There are times when our actions bring needless anguish. There are times when we suffer for our foolishness. It is not all redemptive suffering.

But much of what we suffer is to purify us for the afterlife and when we offer our suffering to Jesus it's *very* powerful.

So is fasting. Fasting and doing penance on earth allow us to elude many sufferings which at some levels of Purgatory can be a state of discomfort comparable to standing all day in wet sand, or like being detained in a small dingy room. It may be like spending months with a sickly feeling.

"Purgatory has levels just like Heaven has levels," said Sondra Abrahams, the Louisiana woman who had the death experience. "It has the lowest level that's closest to Hell, a warm spot. It's not really fires. I hear people say fires are burning you but the fire is *within* the person. It's the burning desire to be with God and to be with Christ. They know where Heaven is. They know they had their opportunity here on earth but they did not take advantage of it to do good and to do His work. You can't enter Heaven without being purified. Purgatory is a sad place. I call it the sad zone. I saw people crying and praying for us. They can't ask anything for themselves. That's why the prayers on earth for them are so important."

Let me repeat as it can't be repeated enough that there are many souls in Purgatory who do not receive prayers. God allows them benefit from the prayers said for other people who are already in Heaven but there is never enough. There is suffering due to a lack of it. This is why we hear of "haunted" homes. This is why we hear of the dead trying to communicate with us. While we have to be careful and stay away from contacting the dead (because demons can disguise themselves as the deceased), there are times when God permits a soul to initiate such contact to remind a living person of the need for prayer.

Many times the only cure for a haunted house is to have a Mass said for whoever is haunting the place. Such souls come to us in dreams. "God can miraculously permit the souls of the faithful departed to manifest themselves to the living for a useful end, and principally in order to manifest some truth or other," said the famous mystical theologian Adolphe Tanqueray. At Medjugorje the Virgin said, *"There are in Purgatory souls who pray ardently to God, but for whom no relative or friend prays on earth. God makes them benefit from the prayers of other people. It happens that God permits them to manifest in different ways, close to their relatives on earth, in order to remind men of the existence of Purgatory and to solicit their prayers to come close to God Who is just but good."*

I remember visiting a relative one day when suddenly, across the room, away from either one of us, a picture of her with her late husband went crashing from one level of the end table to the lower surface. Immediately I was given the impression that this man, who had died about ten years before and happened to be Protestant, was reaching out for prayers. The intuition was intense and my aunt said the picture had never done that before.

Another time I was visiting my parents and while in prayer I suddenly saw a woman frantically waving at me.

It was in my mind's eye but in a way I don't usually see things. It was a woman who had lived up the street from my parents, a woman I didn't know well but who had died some years before and was desperately trying to get my attention.

It was my impression that she needed prayers because she was in acute pain and no one was praying for her.

Chapter 18

Often we hear about cases where ghostly apparitions are seen or where household articles are mysteriously moved in the rooms of those departed. This can be a plea for intercession and we should immediately have a Mass said for whoever it was who lived in the house. We cannot command out human spirits as we can command out demons. Instead, we release them with prayer, pleading with God to lessen their Purgatory or to free them from their earth-bound status.

There are spirits that rise from the body but who, in a state of confusion or unwillingness to leave earth, do not immediately complete their journey through the passage. Something has caused them to become "stuck." They are between the spiritual and physical. They may be overly attached to a person, place, object, or habit of the earthly world.

It was the manifestation of purgatorial souls—crying from a cave in Sicily—that inspired commemoration of the dead on November 2.

Hauntings may also be the sign of a person who has been allowed by God to do his or her Purgatory in earthly surroundings. This was very common around Padre Pio, who once said that more *deceased* people visited him at San Giovanni Rotondo than did the living.

Well-known is the account of how one evening in the early 1920s Pio was praying in the choir loft when he heard a scratching sound coming from below at the side altars.

Listening intently, the famous priest was startled by a second sound, that of a candelabra falling from the main altar.

Leaning over the rail to see who was causing the commotion and supposing it was a student, Pio was surprised to see a young friar at the side of the altar.

When the priest asked what the friar was doing, there was only silence.

Finally Pio demanded the man explain his purpose and the friar gave his name. "I am doing my Purgatory here," he said. "I was a student in this friary, so I now have to make amends for the errors I committed while I was here, for my lack of diligence in doing my duty in this church."

As it turned out, the friar had been in Purgatory sixty years. He was one of many who sought Pio's aid in attaining Heaven.

Another time Pio encountered four deceased friars who were sitting around the fireplace in a state of suffering. The priest prayed that whole night in front of the Blessed Sacrament to free them.

Yet another time after dinner those at the friary heard some voices coming from the downstairs hallway after the friary had been locked. They were shouting, *"Vive Padre Pio!"*

Pio later explained that they were the voices of deceased soldiers who had come to thank him for his prayers, which had released them.

Chapter 19

And so it is that we're all called to pray for the deceased and repeat as often as we can, as frequently as possible, "Oh my Jesus, forgive us our sins, save us from the fires of Hell, lead all souls to Heaven, especially those most in need of Thy mercy."

The mercy of Christ must be begged. It must be beseeched. It must be implored. Recently I was at the side of a dying man who had requested his wife say the Chaplet of Divine Mercy and when he died it was precisely at 3 p.m., the moment of mercy.

Especially powerful for souls is the Rosary and the Way of the Cross. I particularly recommend the Scriptural Rosary and reading the *Psalms*.

Then there is the powerhouse of Mass.

Nothing is as effective as Mass for the departed or departing. Padre Pio dedicated 15 minutes for the dead during his daily liturgy and offered up his incredible suffering.

"Mass is the greatest prayer of God," said the Medjugorje Virgin. *"You will never be able to understand its greatness."*

When a soul in Purgatory has a Mass said for it, it's like a windfall of grace.

It's also important to have Mass said for people while they're alive. We're told this is more effective than having Masses said for them afterwards.

And we should also receive Communion for guidance on how to conduct our own lives and purify ourselves on earth. We should always ask for instruction on how we should conduct ourselves to avoid Purgatory.

And that guidance will come clearest through Mass.

Nothing can compare to praising and receiving Christ.

Every time we participate in the Eucharist we decrease our time in Purgatory.

So powerful is this sacrament, so very potent, that purgatorial spirits would give anything just to come back and spend a single minute, a second, in Adoration.

Chapter 20

No one escapes divine justice and while it can seem intimidating, we should remember that once in Purgatory a soul has been marked for God's Kingdom. The soul is assured of paradise. There is no longer free will and so a soul cannot commit further transgression. It can't fall into damnation.

I get the impression that much of Purgatory, especially as one begins to pass the middle area, maintains aloneness and introspection as the chief sufferings. I felt like I visited such a purgatory when I went to see an elderly woman who seemed to be doing her Purgatory on earth. She had lost a husband a few years before, and although her life had been vibrant and full of friends, now she found herself with virtually no one. The many friends and relatives had all died, and she was no longer capable of walking very far or driving. She was in the beginning stages of dementia, losing her long-term memory to the point where she couldn't remember the name of a person she had known most of her life.

All day, every week, all though the year, this woman sat alone in her apartment, remaining inside for weeks at a time with the solace only of a television she wasn't very good at operating.

It was excruciatingly lonely. Once a week a step-grandson

would stop by with groceries, and a niece from a town 80 miles away would sometimes pick her up for Christmas, but other times she spent holidays alone. She was in solitary confinement and there was such a feeling of emotional pain in her apartment that few could visit but for a few minutes.

The last time I went to see her I realized that the incredibly intense feeling of suffering was because this woman—a dear and kind woman, certainly no great sinner, a church-goer all her life, when she had been able—was being allowed to do her Purgatory while alive.

Chapter 21

It may sound difficult but Purgatory is God's mercy and a soul there, a soul in final expiation, is redeemed by the Blood of Our Savior. It has seen the light. It has seen God. There is great joy in that. There is great joy in knowing that one day it will be with the Almighty.

One day it will go back to the Heaven it glimpsed upon death.

"It is true that the torments of Purgatory are so great that the most acute sufferings of this life cannot compare to them, but the interior satisfaction which is enjoyed is such that no prosperity, no contentment on earth, can equal it," noted St. Francis de Sales. "The souls are in continual union with God. They are perfectly resigned to His Will, or rather, their will is transformed into that of God, so that they cannot will but that which He wills. Indeed, if paradise were to be opened to them, they would precipitate themselves into Hell rather than appear before God with the stains with which they see themselves disfigured. They willingly and lovingly purify themselves, because such is the divine pleasure."

The higher one goes—the farther past middle Purgatory, the more distant from the chambers of suffering and the dingy loneliness—the brighter it gets. Even the aloneness begins to fade. At least that's the impression I get. There is still suffering but it's more bearable. It's not as overt. The pain diminishes. It is more of a mental suffering.

We can only think in metaphors. No one has a clear picture of the afterlife. One can assume that the higher one goes, the more interaction there is with other souls because the higher in Purgatory, the more frequent are the consolations. It nearly becomes pleasant once beyond the gray zone. As Catherine of Genoa said, "I do not believe that it would be possible to find any joy comparable to the joy of a soul in Purgatory except the joy of the blessed in paradise—a joy which continues to increase day by day as God flows in upon the soul more and more. He does this abundantly, according to the measure in which obstacles to His entrance are removed."

The final internal suffering breaks down our remaining pretense and allows God to weed and spade at our deepest levels. The more hardness we've had, the more intensely Christ has to force His way inside us. We may not realize it, but every time throughout life we dislike or hate someone or become jealous and angered we build a layer around our spirits that can harden like cement. It's not just the overt sins that need breaking apart but also the faults in our spirits. If a person is going to church every day and diligently praying the Rosary as well as indulgence prayers but still harboring envy and dislike, that person must purify himself of such faults or face such purification later.

"I will refine them as silver is refined," the Lord says in *Zechariah* 13:9, "and I will test them as gold is tested."

Chapter 22

As the soul ascends through Purgatory, as it enters the upper reaches after so much suffering, it reaches places that, while lacking God's Presence, take on some characteristics of Heaven.

This is the Purgatory of desire. This is the Threshold. This is where many who have been holy, loving, and diligent on earth—but who have unpurged faults—are sent. It is also where souls from the lower reaches eventually ascend. Here one can only imagine the colors that begin to take shape above the gray areas and the more frequent visits from the Virgin Mary, St. Joseph, and St. Michael.

It's a place where there is more happiness than sadness. It's a place of anticipation. It's a place where the spiritual body has been beautified.

In all our life we have never encountered the kind of beauty we will be given as we approach paradise.

It's not Heaven and there is still purification but it's beautiful because souls see the spiritual world. They see angels. They occasionally hear from Christ. They are given knowledge about matters elsewhere in the afterlife or even events on earth when so permitted as the veil scrolls like a curtain between two worlds and God gives the grace to see beyond time and space.

In a book called *Treatise on the Purgatory of St. Patrick*, an English Cistercian monk named H. of Sawtry related the vision of a knight named Owen who was shown a place of flowers, fruit, and grass with an aroma "on whose fragrance he felt he could subsist forever."

It was upper Purgatory. There was no night, no heat, no cold.

Here the final lessons are learned, the final impatience is purged, the last of anger is erased, the tiniest residues of lust and dislike and resentment replaced with total love.

The more a soul loves God, the more a soul loves others, the more beautiful, purified, and radiant it becomes. The Threshold is a place that puts a soft glow on death. "Seen in the light of God, death becomes a sweet encounter," wrote Father Alessio Parente. "It becomes not the sunset but a beautiful dawn, the forerunner to eternal life with God. When the heart is filled with God, death no longer frightens, but it becomes a sweet caress—the caresses of God as He welcomes His creature."

At the upper reaches of Purgatory, at the highest stage, the immediate environment is said to resemble Heaven. There is still pain but there is also a certain peace, comfort, and beauty. No doubt many holy people who had some minor need of purification do their entire purgatories here.

At the high levels souls can probably communicate more readily and pray with less effort than in the oppressive lower levels. I imagine there are many souls at that stage who would have gone directly to Heaven but for a bit too much pride and self-love.

We're told there are souls who would have made the grand entry but didn't have a strong enough desire, while on earth, to see God.

Chapter 23

Now they do. Now they appreciate God for Who and what He is. Now, at the Threshold, there is still the insatiable yearning to see Him, a suffering cruel indeed—the ardent desire which is such a martyrdom—but as Sister O recounted, the soul feels that the end of exile is at hand.

This is the final expiation. As Father F. X. Schouppe pointed out in a well-known book on Purgatory, sin produces the double effect called debt of guilt and debt of pain. After the guilt is pardoned, he points out, "it generally happens that the pain remains to be undergone, either entirely or in part, and this must be endured either in the present life or in the life to come."

We must purge the slightest stain of guilt and debts must be paid on all the faults of life. Such was also taught by St. Catherine of Genoa.

As I said, those who do not have much residue fly right through. Many are the accounts of holy souls who spent but a moment in Purgatory. Make no mistake: Nothing in Purgatory is Heaven. God is still absent. It's no substitute for paradise. There's still that exquisite pain of not having the Divine Vision.

But as the soul goes through final refinement, it's like being in a waiting room and there is a resplendence that becomes similar to that of Heaven.

Often souls at the Threshold need but a few prayers to find their release and so we must pray for them. When we offer our fasting or suffering, and especially when we offer a Mass, it's a *powerful* aid to such souls. When we pray for all the souls in Purgatory, when we say a Rosary for all the poor souls, it's as if that Rosary is being prayed for each one.

Every day we should offer at least a few prayers for those in Purgatory, perhaps setting aside several beads or a decade of the Rosary if not an entire Rosary for their elevation.

We're called to help these souls. We're called to have Masses said for them. We should mention them by name. There is still some suffering. A good practice is having a Mass said once a month or even once a week for someone we know who has died and until we have exhausted the names of all deceased we have ever known.

Every time we pray for a purgatorial soul, according to Medjugorje, that soul can *see* us.

The veil scrolls up.

It's a beautiful thought: they are aware that we're praying, and when it's our time to head for the other side, they will be there to help us.

Those many little pains and sacrifices of daily life we encounter can all be offered for the good of souls, turning every suffering into a gift from God! Especially we should remember those families who don't pray, or who are from a non-Catholic background and don't believe in Purgatory. These souls encounter special distress. For even in the more "pleasant" areas of Purgatory, souls are held accountable, as Christ said (*Matthew* 12:36), "for every unguarded word" they spoke on earth.

Chapter 24

There is thus the final purging of bad habits and faulty ways and attachments of the world.

The soul is refined like polished silver.

When a soul is ready for release such is often conducted by the Virgin and Archangel Michael. "She comes to Purgatory on her feasts and she goes back to Heaven with many souls," Sister O had said. "St. Michael accompanies her. The best and most efficacious way of glorifying him in Heaven and honoring him on earth is to spread devotion to the souls in Purgatory, and to make known the great mission he fulfills towards these suffering souls. Those who have forgotten the holy souls are forgotten in their turn. When God allows it, we can communicate directly with St. Michael in the way that spirits communicate. We see Michael as we see the angels. He has no body. He comes to get the souls that have finished their purification. It is he who conducts them to Heaven. He is the highest angel in Heaven. Our own Guardian Angels come to see us but St. Michael is far more beautiful than they are. As to the Blessed Virgin, we see her in body."

Except for our relation with Jesus, Who we should go to directly, nothing is of more solace than the relation with Mary.

The Blessed Mother is there to assist souls and those souls dedicated to her throughout their lives are specially visited as they are waiting their exit.

When a mystic named Sister Paola di Santa Teresa was in ecstasy one day, she was taken to a purgatory where she saw the Virgin surrounded by a countless retinue of angels who were with her to free the souls.

There is also the role of plenary indulgences. They are not to be despised or neglected. They do work. But to entirely gain them the soul must have the right disposition of will and heart. God permits indulgences according to our dispositions. We receive what God wants us to receive. When a soul is close to Heaven it may take only one well-gained indulgence to tip the balance.

I found it fascinating that both the nun of the Purgatory revelation and the Virgin at Medjugorje both said it is not All Souls' Day but Christmas when the most souls are freed from Purgatory. "On All Souls' Day many souls leave the place of expiation and go to Heaven," said Sister O in the 19th century. "Also, by a special grace of God on that day only, all the suffering souls, without exception, have a share in the public prayers of the Church, even those who are in the great Purgatory. It is not, however, on All Souls' Day that the most go to Heaven. It is on Christmas night."

Compare that with what Mary said at Medjugorje in 1983: *"It is not on All Souls' Day but at Christmas that the greatest number of souls leave Purgatory."*

Chapter 25

In the twinkling of Christmas, as families rejoice, as kids open presents, so do the freed souls rejoice upon entry into a realm of sheer and pure delight. It is paradise. It's the Vision of God. Obviously there's no way I can really describe Heaven. Even those who say they've seen it are at an utter loss for words.

It's extensive. It's infinite. It's bigger than the universe. It goes on forever and has endless aspects and we spend our eternity exploring it.

I think of heavenly paintings. I think of the best landscapes on earth. I think of the beauty of a place like Africa or New Zealand and multiply it infinitely.

For the most gorgeous sight, the most incredible photograph, the most stunning sunset you have seen on earth is but a shadow, a tiny glimmer, of paradise.

I remember once looking out a window at the mountains in Colorado as the sun rose with colors I'd never before seen. It was like my window had become a gorgeous painting. I couldn't believe the sky could have so many hues of blue and red.

But that's nothing compared to Heaven. Earth is only an imitation. The greenest green and the brightest blue would seem dingy in paradise.

Earth is a great gift from God but it absolutely pales compared with our true home, which is Heaven.

And to draw close to it we have to watch over our every thought and offer everything in perfect union with God. He and only He is our chief companion and witness. He is the one we should go to every day for instructions on what to do. We must not be overly attached to anything or anyone of this passing world.

How great is what awaits us! How short and bitter can be life but how glorious is the reward for those who are well tested!

Our entire lives must become prayers if we're to directly gain Heaven, and when we suffer frustration and disappointment, when we suffer trials, we must rise above them.

We must offer them to Jesus.

Chapter 26

We should also meditate on our lives and repair past damage. We should love where before we failed to love. I recommend a novena of Masses for our lives— a Mass for each year we've been alive—and during each Mass, asking God to send love and blessings where we had failed to love and to bless every single person who ever came anywhere near our presence, from the moment of our conceptions to the present.

I believe the power of Mass is unlimited and that if we begin a life novena in which we meditate on a different year of our lives each day, and then offer Mass for it, we can begin the necessary cleansing here on earth.

It should be coupled with regular Confession. I urge people to go to Confession at least once a month and to pray always. Pray for everyone. We're all the children of God. When we help or pray for another person, we help everyone on the planet. There's a chain reaction and God will view us in terms of how we carried out our role in that chain reaction. As I've said, the seemingly insignificant people with quiet roles may have more of an effect than those we think of as "movers and shakers."

The quiet housewife raising her children and praying well

may well affect the universe more than a politician or author.

We have no idea what we have done until we see our lives through the Light of Christ, and while we're on earth we must constantly keep that evaluation before us, praying that we conduct our lives right now as if we are already privy to the way our lives will look from the other side.

We must constantly invoke the Holy Spirit to let us know what we should do with each hour of our lives. We must give to God right now all the remaining sufferings and good acts of our lives, so that not a day is wasted when we reach the judgment.

Chapter 27

And we must always ask: What does Jesus want from me? Who am I in His eyes? Who does He want me to be?

We start by practicing love. We should see goodness in others. That begins the process. If there's one common theme among those who have glimpsed the other side, it is that *love* is the final measure. In the end, much of life reduces to how much we have loved, and that means not just those in our families, not just relatives and friends, but our neighbors and coworkers and everyone we happen upon through life, even antagonists and total strangers.

One day we may learn that there was more goodness in others than we realized and that we should have loved more intently.

Love is patient. Love is kind. Love is wishing everyone the best. Love is putting others first. Love is healing through the spirit. Love is touching our fellow man at the deepest level of existence and it is allowing Jesus to enlarge and take over our hearts.

Pray for Jesus to enter. Pray for Him to soften your hearts. Pray for Him to give you the great love that only He can give, because love is the real ticket to Heaven.

We should ask God to purge us of the residue from every major and minor sin. We should ask the Lord to show us what we need to attain perfection. We should assume that we are very imperfect. We should ask for examples of how we can better conduct ourselves and most importantly we should unite in love with Jesus.

During the Eucharist we break any bonds that set upon us during each year of our lives, and we plead His blood over every minute of our lives to purify and relieve us of all evil.

A mortified life is to be desired much more than a life of mystical gifts, for true sanctity consists in renouncing oneself, in constantly putting aside the ego, in allowing God to work in and with us as He wills, and to receive the graces He sends with profound humility. Had they to do it over again, souls in Purgatory would orient each day in seeking to be who God wanted them to be. They would pray to know what God wants of them. They would pray to know His will. They would meditate on who they are and who God wants them to be. They would detach themselves from all earthly things and make sure to put God far above any earthly creatures.

All must be done for God. There must be perfection. There must be indifference to everything except that which is for the Father. One must reproduce in his or her soul the conduct of Jesus. We must detach from ourselves. We must realize that earth is a place of suffering and tests and we must pass through that exile without complaint. We must rise above all earthly things, all self-love or inordinate passion, and lose ourselves totally in His will.

Every day we should pray that God's designs be fulfilled in us and that we never place any obstacles in the way of His plan.

We must be united with Jesus. We must totally replace our hearts with His. We must strive never to lose sight of Him, not even for a moment.

We must unite entirely.

We should pray that we desire what Jesus wills. We should let Him completely take over our hearts. We should do everything night and day for Him and Him alone. We should give up self-will for His Will and self-love for His love.

We must enlarge our hearts so that Christ can find His love in it. We must love God with the pure fervent affection of a child.

Chapter 28

That's the ticket, the last fare, into paradise.

Said Jesus in *Matthew* 18:4, "Whoever makes himself lowly, becoming like this child, is of greatest importance in that Heavenly reign."

"I assure you that whoever does not accept the reign of God like a little child shall not take part in it," He added in *Mark* 10:15.

Heaven is God and God is love and those who seek it must have a child's pure and innocent love.

Our lives must be spent for God.

He must consume our thoughts.

Our lives must be spent breaking down our superficial egos and striving instead, working tirelessly, at attaining His Vision.

Nothing matters but God, Who is all.

If we have love and concern ourselves with Him, we concern ourselves with everyone.

The things we think are great things are minor in the light of eternity.

The only significance is God's Light.

And what a light it is!

If everyone who has ever experienced or written about

Heaven, including those who wrote the Bible, could agree on one thing, it's that Heaven exceeds our wildest expectations.

Heaven is better than anything we can imagine because it's way beyond earth's choicest pleasures.

Heaven is the best moment in our lives multiplied thousands of times.

Every moment in Heaven is better than the best moment we have spent on earth.

Heaven is exquisite beyond exquisite because the soul is in direct contact with its Creator. It's in the constant Presence of Jesus. It's surrounded by angels in a sea of the Holy Spirit, a sea of peace, joy, and well-being.

It's like taking Communion every minute of every hour of every day.

When I speak to those who have had death experiences, I'm struck by the consistent joy that registers. You see it on their faces, in their words, in their smiles.

Anyone who has touched Heaven never forgets the feeling. They're touching something that cannot be duplicated in worldly life. It can't be imitated.

Throughout history men have tried. Men have tried to bring Heaven to the world. Men have used their money to build huge castles and glittery banquet rooms and verdant landscapes. They have invented the nicest perfumes and have developed elaborate ways of preparing food. They've used silver for their utensils and gilded their buildings with gold. They've chosen the most picturesque of settings near mountains and sea and have surrounded themselves with servants. They have invented the most convenient possible means of travel and communication and have the finest of jewels and clothing.

Yet the richest man on earth, the greatest multi-billionaire in history, the most inventive tycoon on the planet can't come anywhere near replicating the beauty and perfection of Heaven

—and in trying to create paradise is actually that much farther from the real thing.

As it says again in *1 Corinthians* 2:9, "Eye has not seen, ear has not heard, nor has it so much as dawned on man what God has prepared for those who love Him."

That love is the task before all of us for the rest of our lives. This very moment should be for us the first minute of a different path. It's the path of Heaven. It's the path of eternity. It's the path, more than all else, of love.

No matter what you have done or haven't done in your lives, no matter how far you have been from God, no matter how imperfect you have been in your devotions, you have the opportunity right now to change everything in the direction of paradise.

You have the opportunity to change your heart into the shape of the Eucharist.

That means going to Mass. That means understanding the fantastic proportions of the liturgy. Heaven is like being in a constant state of receiving Communion and we touch paradise every time we attend Mass. We take a step to Heaven—often a big step—with each Confession or visit to the Blessed Sacrament.

It's there that God speaks to our hearts and lets us know what we should do and how we should do it to attain Heaven. Mass gives us a taste of Heaven because it's attended by many saints and angels and opens a porthole to the eternal.

Each day we must love God more than the day before. Each day we must meditate on our love for Him. Each day we should exercise this love and develop this love by *praising* Him.

Throughout the day we should say "Praise you, God," over and over. "Praise you, Holy Spirit. Praise you, Jesus." We should praise Him in our own way and also by reading the *Psalms*. We should praise Him by reading the Bible. And we should thank Him. We should endlessly thank the Lord. We should thank Him for His goodness. We should thank Him for creating us. We should thank Him for protecting us all these years. We should thank Him for our parents and our spouses and our homes. We should thank Him for allowing us to live this long. We should thank Him for drawing us from so many dangerous situations in life. We should thank Him for His forgiveness. We should thank Him for His mercy.

Praising and thanking Jesus brings us in unity with Him, and that's what we must persistently seek: the love flowing from Christ and the rays of His enormous loving kindness.

We should hug Him. We should feel drawn up to His great power as we are assisted by all the angels and saints. We should feel close to the Virgin. We must remain in her embrace.

And we should speak to Christ with the simplicity of a child. We should feel the thoughts come not from our brains but from our hearts. It's crucial to open up our hearts. It's crucial to feel love for Jesus as He pours out His mercy, which we further increase by reciting the Chaplet of Divine Mercy.

Implore Him. Implore His mercy. Love His mercy. Adore His mercy. Adore Christ as you have never adored anything or anyone, adore His life, adore His suffering, adore His triumph over evil and you will feel His presence.

Love Christ and offer Him every little suffering. When we suffer well, we greatly diminish Purgatory. Every little suffering is a gift from Christ because it's an opportunity. It's an opportunity to join with His own suffering and to purify our lives.

When suffering is borne patiently it loses its sting and it is powerful when united with any penances we choose, especially fasting, which is a tremendously potent means of earthly purgation. Fasting gives us clear vision and a clean soul and all day that must be our vocation: cleansing. When we're taking a shower or washing our faces, we should ask God to cleanse our spirits as we are cleansing our bodies. When we breathe we should inhale the Holy Spirit as we inhale air and when we encounter any little difficulty whatsoever, we should immediately offer it up to Heaven and indeed announce every morning that all the sufferings the rest of our lives are offered for the love of God!

Chapter 29

We can pray with a simple word: "Jesus." We can pray by sending love. Our best prayer is love of God and love of others. We should seek to serve others and pray for such opportunities. Pray to God to see how you can help other souls attain Heaven. Pray to help souls in Purgatory. Kneel often in front of the Crucifix and conduct everything in your life as if you are always in church. Use indulgences. Say the prayers that have been given you. And tend to the little things in life. St. Therese the Little Flower said it's the little everyday things that get us to Heaven. You don't have to be dramatic. Offer God your small mortifications. Fast from every and any impurity. Be good and loving to all. This is powerful stuff and brings us to Heaven in combination with holy Mass and visits to the Blessed Sacrament.

Use the sacraments. Use the prayers. Bless your house. Clean it spiritually. Protect yourself with holy water. Use anointed oil. Pray in your idle moments instead of thinking thoughts that are gossipy or meaningless. Wear the brown Scapular. The promise of Our Blessed Mother to St. Simon Stock was that anyone wearing the Scapular *"shall not suffer eternal fire."*

The Little Office of the Virgin Mary should go with the

Scapular; and never forget the Rosary. Every *Hail Mary* is worth time off Purgatory.

Pray to the Blessed Mother. Pray for constant guidance of your angels and saints. Give alms in honor of the holy souls. Pray always for the deceased. And most importantly, remove anything in your lives that may lead to Purgatory. Review not only your sins but also your bad habits. Ask the Holy Spirit to let you see with the eyes of Christ and He will come like a dove to prepare your way.

We are only well-equipped when we have kindness and knowledge. These survive the grave.

That's why it's important to learn.

That's why it's far more important to have knowledge than money.

The material things don't come with us but what we have learned is ours forever.

Are we still men and women once we die?

There are debates about this but from what I can tell the majority of mystical writings indicate that there may be no more gender. We still have our identities but are no longer male or female. We are pure spirits. That's what many believe. I don't pretend to know. Do we become like angels? In at least some cases, it seems that once it's purified, a soul may have the mission of watching and helping those who are still on earth. There are echelons in Heaven and wisemen and holy souls who have certain roles and jurisdictions.

The words of Sondra echo in my ears: "Heaven is so beautiful. I can't describe. There's the most beautiful music, and people are happy there. There are angels everywhere."

As the cop in Omaha said, he realized there are "just no big deals in this world. I knew I would just love the Lord and do what's right!"

We'll be shocked when we reach Heaven at how seemingly minor things were great things if we did them for God. The greatness lies in whether we did it for God or for ourselves.

The greatness is in the eternal mission.

The greatness—the judgment—will be in how much love was behind it, not just love of fellow man but above all love of the eternal Trinity.

Chapter 30

Heaven is beyond human comprehension. Time after time we hear of the beauty. Time after time we hear it said that those in Heaven are in a state of complete satisfaction. They are at the highest level of well-being. They are consumed by a love that goes far beyond any love you have ever felt. They are happy. They're beyond happy. The joy they feel is a normal and constant state. There's no more pain. There's no more suffering. There's no more tending to a body. There is no more worry over money. There is no more need for clothes or living quarters and there's no more loneliness. In Heaven souls love each other with a love unknown in the bondage of earthly life and are united with those who have preceded them.

What do visionaries say about Heaven? At Medjugorje they described a vast space with a brilliant light that never wavers. A light that never fades. A light that is not reflected off objects so much as radiating from them. It's like nothing of the earth. Nor are the colors. In brilliancy, texture, and variability the colors are beyond earthly colors. The most beautiful color of earth, the most incredible azure, is but a shadow of Heavenly azure. Everything on earth is a mere shadow. The people are often seen by visionaries as wearing pink, gray, or yellow robes and this is also the way those who experienced death have described them: robes that are really like nothing of this world but described like pastel.

There is music. There is Heavenly music. It too is like nothing on earth. The music is from an actual choir of angels and it's a beautiful, calming music, an exalting music, a sound that constantly praises God.

There are exquisite aromas. The smells are also beyond earth. And then there are the meetings with loved ones.

"I saw my grandmother whom I had never met," said Sondra. She died way before I was born. She was just smiling. I remember her saying the Rosary. I had never met her, but I *knew* her. There were some buildings. Everything was in gold and silver and jewels. Everything radiated. And the smell—oh! Everything was in a beautiful mist. There's no way you're going to want to stand before God with even a little blemish. Heaven is so beautiful you don't want to dirty it in any way with anything on your soul. There were people taking care of babies in a nursery-like place. You know who they are but they don't look like you and me.

"I remember turning and the Blessed Mother was there and she's absolutely beautiful. I always thought I was insignificant, but she knew me. She had heard all of my prayers. And Christ showed me the angels they had sent to me when I needed someone.

"The people in Heaven sing. They do have jobs to do. I don't know what they were doing but they were all very busy and they were all so *happy*! Everyone was dressed the same, something long, white, pink, blue, like robes. They seemed all the same age, in their twenties or thirties. Here was my grandmother who looked so young and radiant.

"I saw a little bit of the throne of God. I wasn't allowed to see God and I know why. I won't be able to until He judges me one day. If the little part of the throne of God I saw is any indication of the size of God Himself, He's *huge*, and the angels I saw kneeling there praising and singing to Him were huge—*huge*—and I could only see a little tiny part of His chair."

Another person, a Christian physician named Richard Eby, encountered "gorgeous, white, four-petaled flowers" and Heavenly music that was beautifully different from anything we know. "In a twinkling I discovered why," he said. "It had no beat, and it came from everywhere. I also noted that my white gown, besides emitting a pure white light, was singing softly—as was my body, the flowers, trees, hills and sky" (see *1 Chronicles* 16:31-33).

When Dr. Eby asked why the music had no beat, he was told it was because in Heaven there's no time to divide into beats!

The doctor also recorded a delicate aroma (an exquisite fragrance that reminds us of the "odor of sanctity") and found his body to be transparent and self-illuminated—weightless and cloudlike. His robe felt rare and like silk. "For miles it seemed, there stretched rolling hills under cloudless skies of a color new to me, of an iridescent white-gold light," he wrote in a book about his experience with Jesus. "Flawless evergreens covered the hills which rose from the flower-carpeted valley floor. The trees somewhat resembled arborvitae but were too stately and perfect to be earthly."

He said the grass "grew thickly and without a single broken blade."

This is remarkably similar to an ancient description by Pope Gregory of the man Stephen who after crossing the bridge over foul water encountered "delightful meadows carpeted with green grass and sweet-smelling flowers. The meadows seemed to be meeting places for people clothed in white. Such a pleasant odor filled the air that the sweet smell by itself was enough to satisfy the inhabitants who were strolling there. In that place each one had his own separate dwelling, filled with magnificent light."

There are blue skies and lakes and a mixed panoply of flowers, everything gold or silver. People look very, very happy, for Heaven is filled with immense light and everyone wears a constant smile. When there are buildings, they don't seem to have barriers or walls. There is what seems like marble but no real stone. We cannot imagine this in physical terms. There are landscapes but they're not physical. They're boundless. Everything seems like diamonds and stars and at Medjugorje there were similar descriptions. Heaven was described as a place where people are always singing with angels hovering above and the happiness on the faces such that it goes beyond depiction.

People in Heaven know the absolute fullness, said Vicka, of a created being.

"The trees, the meadows, the sky are totally different from anything on the earth," added Mirjana. "And the light is much more brilliant. Heaven is beautiful beyond any possible comparison with anything I know of on earth. (The people) were walking in a beautiful park. They have everything. They need or want nothing. They are totally full."

Chapter 31

To the soul in Heaven, the earth seems like a mere speck next to the vast unending horizons of eternity.

"There are ever new feasts which succeed each other without interruption," said Sister O. "There is happiness, always new and such, it would seem, as has never been enjoyed. It is a torrent of joy which flows unceasingly over the elect. Heaven is above and beyond all—GOD: God loved, God relished, God delighted in."

Beautiful are the many descriptions by mystics of the way Mary conducts souls to Heaven. They look like sparks of ascending radiance.

Mary is the Queen of Heaven and so we must implore her help in getting to that incredible place where all sorrows are forgotten, all anxiety disappears, all sadness is erased. Mystics have described incredible waterfalls and the sparkling gemlike buildings of an eternal city.

As one man who experienced death put it, "all of us are mysteriously connected to each other forever in a universe of such vast beauty that words cannot possibly describe it."

There are those who recount the spectacular valleys, the gardens with flowers that seem to sway to celestial music, the living fountains and the symphony of sounds in a place where the sweetest conceivable music praises God.

In Heaven objects are real and yet unreal, ephemeral and yet more authentic than anything of the earth, filled with people whose love spills upon every new entrant and who seek in every way to help.

Life comes from the water and trees and gardens. Heaven is ornamented with the colors of jewels mined from the empyrean. If you can imagine a place filled only with the best friends you have ever had in your life, filled with those who had loved you sincerely and the most, those who wished you only the best, then multiply that many times and you have the essence of Heaven, which is the essence of love.

Love radiates. Love sings. Love permeates the atmosphere. Love *is* the atmosphere. Love is God and God is Heaven and those who are in Heaven are there because they have learned to shed their egos and to direct everything from the bottom of their souls to the cause of eternal love.

There's no jealousy in Heaven. There is no wanting attention. There is no envy. There is no wishing ill upon others but instead a perfect congruence—a perfect harmony—and such an immaculate surrounding that anyone with so much as a speck would not want to enter the incredible Kingdom.

"I want each one of you to be happy here on earth and to be with me in Heaven," said the Virgin of Medjugorje. *"That is, dear children, the purpose of my coming here and it's my desire. Peace, peace, peace. Only peace. Make your peace with God and among yourselves. For that, it is necessary to believe, to pray, to fast, and to go to Confession. Whoever has done very much evil during his life can go straight to Heaven if he confesses, is sorry for what he has done, and receives Communion at the end of his life."*

It's a small number who go directly to Heaven but they do

so if they have been able to turn into perfect faith, humility, and love. They do so if they have been absolved of all sin. And that again raises the crucial topic of Confession. Invoking the Holy Spirit, we ask God in the name of Jesus to enlighten us as to how and what we should confess, so there is not a speck of unsightliness.

When we ask the Holy Spirit to come, He arrives to indicate the hidden corners of our souls and to show us what we in our spiritual blindness can't or don't want to see.

Come Holy Spirit! Come and enlighten our souls! Come and lead us to Heaven!

There is no more relevant prayer. Every moment on earth is a precious opportunity for attaining Heaven. Every moment is an opportunity for prayer and love. It's only when our very lives become a prayer that we have unity with Christ and only then do we have the sure route to paradise and its golden gates, its shining cities, its seraphic choirs.

Then and only then can we approach the fantastic light, the incredible and infinitely powerful light, the never-ending and never-described Light that is the Vision of God.

Notes

Chapters 1-5: The Bible I use is mainly the *New American Bible* published by Thomas Nelson Inc. in Camden, N.J. *The Catechism of the Catholic Church* is published by Liberia Editrice Vaticana. I also use a computer Bible manufactured by Franklin Electronic Publishers (Mount Holly, New Jersey). The quotes on death patients are from a study called "Deathbed Observations by Physicians and Nurses" by Karlis Osis (privately published in New York). For Gallup see *Adventures in Immortality* by George Gallup, Jr. (New York: McGraw-Hill Book Company, 1982). The figure on belief in afterlife comes from the Catholic News Service. The account of the physician who left his body is from *Beyond Death's Door* by Dr. Maurice Rawlings (New York: Bantam Books, 1979). For the quote from the Yale doctor see page 68 of the March 1992 issue of *Life Magazine*, which was also the source for the Balducci quote. The account of the woman from Bismarck comes from *The Journey Home* by Phillip L. Berman (New York: Pocketbooks, 1996), which is also the source for the Heim quote. For the sense of well-being, see page 106 of *Otherworld Journeys* by Carol Zaleski (Oxford: Oxford University Press, 1987), which was also the source (page 125) for the quote from the man who nearly "floated" in God's light.

Michael H. Brown

For Vicka's quote see page 62 of *Queen of the Cosmos* by Jan Connell (Orleans, Massachusetts: Paraclete Press, 1990).

Chapters 6-10: For the accounts of St. Clare, St. Stanislaus, and St. Hyacinth, see *Visions of Mary* by Peter Eicher (New York: Avon Books, 1996). For the Ritchie quote see his book *Return from Tomorrow* (Waco, Texas: Chosen Books, 1978). For St. Salvius and Drythelm see *Otherworld Journeys* and also the saints' biographies in *Butler's Lives of Saints* (Allen, Texas: Christian Classics). For Reginald Garrigou-Lagrange see his book *Life Everlasting* (Rockford, Illinois: TAN Publishers, 1991). For the Idaho woman, the Heim account of a mountain climber, and the man who nearly drowned, see *Otherworld Journeys*. The account from Medjugorje comes from a June 15, 1995, faxed report by Sister Emmanuel, a nun stationed there. For Marija Pavlovic's quotes see pages 120 and 121 of *Queen of the Cosmos*. The Garrigou-Lagrange quote is from *Life Everlasting*, previously cited. For Sister Lucia's quote on Hell see page 104 of *Fatima in Lucia's Own Words*, edited by Father Louis Kondor (Fatima, Portugal: Postulation Centre). This is also the source for the quote from Francisco (page 138). For the quotes from Our Lady of Medjugorje see *Words from Heaven* (Birmingham, Alabama: Saint James Publishing, 1990). For Hell see Dr. Rawlings's *Beyond Death's Door* (previously cited) and *To Hell and Back* (Nashville: Thomas Nelson Publishers, 1993). For the art professor see *The Journey Home*, page 88, previously cited. The figure of five in forty comes from psychotherapist Margot Grey and her book *Return From Death* (New York: Arcana Press, 1985). Abbe Chatel's quote comes from the January-February 1988 issue of *Soul* Magazine, which quotes his book, published in 1987 but unavailable in English. For St. Teresa of Avila see *The Life of Teresa of Avila* (New York: Image Books, 1960).

Chapters 11-15: For Bible references see *Beginning Apologetics* by Father Frank Chacon and Jim Burnham (St. Joseph Radio, Orange County, California). See also Father John Hampsch's book *Healing Your Family Tree*, from which I draw some of the information on Scriptural references (Los Angeles: Claretian Tape Ministry, 1986). For the quote from Drythelm see *Purgatory* by Father F. X. Schouppe (Rockford, Illinois: Tan Books and Publishers, 1983), page 43 (also spelled "Drithelm"). The quote from Angie Fenimore is from her book *Beyond the Darkness* (New York: Bantam Books, 1995). For Dr. Rodonaia see *The Journey Home*. For Sister O and purgatory see "An Unpublished Manuscript On Purgatory" which is available by contacting The Reparation Society of the Immaculate Heart of Mary, 8006 Caliburn Court, Pasadena, Maryland 21122-6438 or calling 410-360-1817. I thank them for permission to use extended quotes, some of which are composite. For Margaret Mary see *The Autobiography of Saint Margaret Mary* (Rockford, Illinois: TAN Publishers), page 110.

Chapters 16-20: For the Jan Connell quote see page 208 of her book *Visions of the Children* (New York: St. Martin's Press, 1992). See also her book *Queen of the Cosmos* (Orleans, Massacusetts: Paraclete Press, 1990), from which comes the Vicka quote on lonely souls. For Marija and purgatory see also "The Blue Letter," a newsletter issued by The Riehle Foundation in Milford, Ohio, August, 1992, and the *Words From Heaven* book previously cited. The quote here is a composite of two quotes. For Tanqueray see "Compendio di Teologia Ascetica e Mistica," page 913. For the Pio accounts as well as the commemoration of November 2, I mainly used *The Holy Souls* by Father Alessio Parente (published by Our Lady of Grace Capuchin Friary in San Giovanni Rotondo, Italy, 1990).

Chapters 21-31: The Parente book is also the source for the quotes from St. Francis de Sales (page 165) and St. Catherine of Genoa (page 28). The quote from Father Schouppe is from his book *Purgatory*, previously cited, pages 111-112; this book is also the source for St. Catherine. For Sister O see again *An Unpublished Manuscript on Purgatory* (phone 410-360-1817 or write The Reparation Society of the Immaculate Heart of Mary, 8006 Caliburn Court, Pasadena, Maryland 21122-6438). For Mirjana's quote see *Queen of the Cosmos*, pages 26-27. The quote on the beauty of heaven comes from page 21 of *The Journey Home*, cited previously. The accounts of Stephen by Pope Gregory and the Knight Owen are from *Otherworld Journeys*. For Dr. Eby see his book *Jesus Told Me to Tell Them I Am Coming* (Old Tappan, New Jersey: Fleming H. Revell Company).

Inspiring New Release!

Seven Days With Mary
by Michael H. Brown

For years we have heard about apparitions. For years we have discerned signs and wonders. Now comes this book of devotion based on the most ancient and solid of Mary's historic apparitions. Every apparition used in this book has been formally approved by the Roman Catholic Church.

Taking one of Mary's appearance for each day of the week, author Michael H. Brown explains their often hidden aspects and offers prayers and meditations to go along with each one, a week of prayers aimed at bringing a week of "special graces." When you finish this book you will experience a feeling of peace and greater lover for the mother of Jesus.

112 pgs.   **$6.50 U.S.   (Canada $10.50)**
ISBN: 1-880033-26-7

FAITH
PUBLISHING
COMPANY

Faith Publishing Company has been organized as a service for the publishing and distribution of materials that reflect Christian values and, in particular, the teachings of the Catholic Church.

It is dedicated to the publication of only those books, flyers, prayer cards, pamphlets, etc. that reflect such values.

Faith Publishing Company also publishes books for The Riehle Foundation, its non-profit, tax-exempt affiliate.

For more information on the publications of Faith Publishing Company, contact:

Faith Publishing Company
P. O. Box 237
Milford, Ohio 45150-0237 USA
513-576-6400

THE
RIEHLE
FOUNDATION

The Riehle Foundation is a non-profit, tax-exempt, charitable organization that exists to produce and/or distribute Catholic material to anyone, anywhere.

The Foundation is dedicated to the Mother of God and her role in the salvation of mankind. We believe that this role has not diminished in our time, but, on the contrary has become all the more apparent in this the era of Mary as recognized by Pope John Paul II, whom we strongly support.

During the past years the Foundation has distributed books, films, rosaries, bibles, etc. to individuals, parishes, and organizations all over the world. Additionally, the Foundation sends materials to missions and parishes in a dozen foreign countries.

Donations forwarded to The Riehle Foundation for the materials distributed provide our sole support. We appreciate your assistance, and request your prayers.

> IN THE SERVICE OF JESUS AND MARY
> All for the honor and glory of God!

The Riehle Foundation
P.O. Box 7
Milford, OH 45150-0007 USA
513-576-0032